for you _____ dy,

Never Before

hugs & true
affection and awe
in & for your passion
for writing!

Laura Anne

11/05

Also by Laure-Anne Bosselaar

The Hour Between Dog and Wolf
(poetry) BOA Editions

Small Gods of Grief
(poetry) BOA Editions

Night Out:
Poems about Hotels, Motels, Restaurants and Bars,
Edited by Kurt Brown & Laure-Anne Bosselaar
Milkweed Editions

Outsiders:
Poems about Rebels, Exiles and Renegades
Edited by Laure-Anne Bosselaar
Milkweed Editions

Urban Nature:
Poems about Wildlife in the City
Edited by Laure-Anne Bosselaar
Milkweed Editions

Forthcoming:

The Plural of Happiness
by Herman de Coninck
Translated by Laure-Anne Bosselaar and Kurt Brown
Field Translation Series, Oberlin College Press, 2006

Never Before:

Poems about First Experiences

An Anthology Edited by
Laure-Anne Bosselaar

Four Way Books
New York City

Distributed by
University Press of New England
Hanover and London

Editorial Office
Four Way Books
POB 535, Village Station
New York, NY 10014
www.fourwaybooks.com

Library of Congress Catalogue Card Number: 2004101062

ISBN 1-884800-60-2

Cover design and illustration: Pablo A. Medina / Cubanica

This book is manufactured in the United States of America and printed on acid-free paper.

Four Way Books is a not-for-profit organization. We are grateful for the assistance we receive from individual donors, foundations, and government arts agencies.

Distributed by University Press of New England
One Court Street, Lebanon, NH 03766

Acknowledgments

My love to you, Martha Rhodes, and my thanks for trusting me with this anthology—my "First Experience"—and a wonderful one—with Four Way Books.

Warm gratitude to Hannah Baker-Siroty, Shannon Tamsin, and Joel Aure, my students at the Sarah Lawrence College MFA in Creative Writing program, for their time, commitment and enthusiasm in helping me with hours and hours of typing and collating.

I am most thankful to Sarah Lawrence College for their generous help in supporting the research and editing of this project.

And to all the poets—as well as many kind publishers—who so generously waived the permission fees: it's thanks to you that this book is in the world. Thank you!

For you, Martha

CONTENTS

TWO

FOUR

Never Before

Never before
have I gone down
on my hands and knees
and begged the earth to stop turning
in its burning sleep
Never before have I asked the sky
why the rain no longer smears
the eyes of this blind house
why the day never again wakens
with the old washed clarity
in which the green new oranges
bob in their rough skins
toward winter and the coming year
Never before
have I turned my whole road
homeward to this one heart
and asked why I am cinders
why I stand in the dawn winds
and cannot smell the coming of day
why I see the white lip of the Pacific
curling back from land and want
to fall through the centuries of unchartered water
toward the frozen center
Will the grass answer
if I bow to it
it is late in the year
and it blows in the autumn chill
blond and careless
the flag of no one
turning slowly to straw or weed
burning in the wasted lot of my life
Never before
have I gone back to the place where I began
and found miles of scattered buildings
rags that were clothes, broken bottles
dishes, yards of burned tires

hills of broken fans, tired motors
dogs, the rubble of lives
that were not lives
and found my own home gone, so much space
filled with the yellow air
we must not breathe
Never before
have I seen in the dark eyes
of children a flame growing slowly
that will scorch first their own hair
and then turn my eyes to fire
never before have I been afraid
as they stood close and not touching
watching me turn back
toward my car and drive away
until the winds whispered stop
and I could sit for a moment
remembering what it was
to rise slowly to a world
that seemed at peace on the long
Sunday mornings of lonely first manhood
when I knew nothing
except there was no work that day
When I ask that man
why he wakened in the dark
and dressed himself in the same dirty clothes
that lay on the floor
and drank only cold water
he answers *Monday*
as though that meant
a basket of fresh laundry before his door
or the soil wakening in long rows
to the tiny fists of new shoots
and not the slam of iron on iron
the hands chewing themselves
to rags of blood and loose skin
Never before
have I heard my own voice
cry out in a language not mine
that the earth was wrong

that night came first and then nothing
that birds flew only to their deaths
that ice was the meaning of change
that I was never a child
nor were you nor were my lost sons
not the sons they won't have
Never before
has dawn streaked the sky
with the purple wastes of iron
has noon turned in the shadows
of small circles of fallen gray leaves
has evening seen the cows
refuse to return
to their long glowing sheds
they shake, they drop their heads
because they must
the hillsides are rusting
the rocks tumble down
so many dull lumps that shatter
into clods of slag
climb higher while the light
still holds out
there is the valley where we came
to rest after turning through water
through the generations of earth, through fire
there is the last dust
rising toward the sun
Never before
have our whole lives
danced in the slow light
of the last hour
never before have I taken
your hand and found
five soiled pages
never before have I taken my own
and found something I had not seen
blood that was heavy and slow
tarnished skin smelling like old breath
bones that laughed
my right arm is

a river that runs toward the heart
bearing no wish
no hope no memory
a river without a name
that began nowhere
and soon will turn back
upon itself
my eyes are deserts
where nothing is
except the dust clouds gathering
far off in another place
until the sun pales
and they are overhead
and must burn
Never before
has the night come down
around me with the blinking
of an eye and the darkness
spread from me to hide it all
the hills behind me
and the scattered used-up farms below
the stale fields, the one horse
broken and old
already hidden in shadow
the old men womenless since birth
walking the roads
their hands folded behind them
their heads down and hatless
their voices at the old familiar prayers
that they will come back
never or to something else
Never before
have they stumbled on and on
in a language
I have forgotten
bowing and rising over
and over, so many stunted
roadside trees burning
as they hold on
and bearing nothing

ONE

When I Was Conceived

It was 1945, and it was May.
White crocus bloomed in St. Louis.
The Germans gave in but the war shoved on,
and my father came home from work that evening
tired and washed his hands
not picturing the black-goggled men
with code names fashioning an atomic bomb.
Maybe he loved his wife that evening.
Maybe after eating she smoothed his jawline
in her palm as he stretched out
on the couch with his head in her lap
while Bob Hope spoofed Hirohito on the radio
and they both laughed. My father sold used cars
at the time, and didn't like it,
so if he complained maybe she held him
an extra moment in her arms,
the heat in the air pressing between them,
so they turned upstairs early that evening,
arm in arm, without saying anything.

First Haircut

You are perched on a padded board
on the arms of the barber's chair, your curls
adrift on the floor, your mother quietly
twisting her blue handkerchief
as you sit face-to-face and back-to-back
in the mirrors forever, your new forehead shining.
Does she see your father, hers, his father
in the glass, back and back in the long room
where you sit in your sheet and tissue collar
while the barber clips you bare?

Why remember it now, fifty years
after, sitting across from her doctor
and signing a paper? Is it the white room?
Is it the deep, secret delight that you
are the last alive? When the nurse lays
the gold wedding band on the desk and you read
the initials inside and the room
smells of bleach and alcohol,
your mother wrapped in a sheet, the barber
spinning his chair, shaking a towel, why
think now of the mirrors that travel forever?

Poem on the First Day of School

All night the priestesses of wisdom have been practicing
the orders I remember of obedience,
silence and devotion to their measured tones,
index fingers hushed across their lips.
Consequently, it is pointless to inform them, half-asleep
as I appear, arriving with my son,
how tiny I am in my own eyes, giving him up
to their language, a guide through fifth grade.
Now he must learn to mouth it as if it were a tongue
by which the world is formed. And he must take a second one
from such images as boys his age barter among themselves
that his words assume their sounds, therefore his own.
I remember. This is how it's done.
This is how I was given to the world.

Waterfall

The creek's easy purr
Under the watchful oaks
Of our home ravine
Challenged, in its calm,
The five-year-olds we were.
We had to find some rocks.
No grit to be seen,
Just cold clammy leather
Ooze from last year's green.
Scavenging on all fours,
Knees soaking, fingers numb,
We came upon sufficient
Granulated, coarse
Marl to jam together.
We watched the meager flow
Tongue backward and stop
Into an undreamt pond,
Then pile against the low
Blockade until it found
The cracks and spilled with a noise
Tiny, new, and ours.
Neither of us grew up
To engineer cement,
To allocate, to sluice
Through soy, to sizzle juice
Through ramifying grids
To urbs from which a whole
Fraternity returned
To skim, to ski, to revel.
No, we were just kids,
Judy and I, intent
On the initial trick,
Meddling with no more use
Than sculptors or even animal
Trainers who teach some pet
To jump over a stick
And catch, midair, the light.

Bridges

My first bridge was a log—a slippery one across a muddy creek
I think my father was trying to teach me something about life
A rickety scrap lumber bridge that led to our railroad cabin
Taught me something of death—my three-year-old nephew
Fell through the railing striking his head on a brace
Probably dead before he hit the shallow stream's surface
Taught me, a twelve-year-old, as I tried to save him, that
I did not have the power of life over death
The logging trestle I walked crossing a wooded canyon
In a deep night was supposed to teach me character.... Did it?
The mythic Golden Gate partially eaten by fog is not real
My most memorable bridge is the one over Lake Pontchatrain
Its lesson one of ennui, that life can be unimpressive
The bridge's plainness what we see, what we are
Its persistent length an ode...

Window of Our Soul

When Sister Maria told us to cut
  the window of our soul
on the thick construction paper
  and then lift it to peer in,
twenty-one second-graders sat
  at our desks
moving the squares of paper up,
  then down, and up again,
and I'd be lying if I told you that
  I saw nothing
but Ann Harding and Tommy Ryan
  two rows ahead—
that the window lifted only on the huge,
  wooden cross
and the still flag, or just the blackboard
  where nine planets
revolved around a black sun,
and I'd be foolish to mention
  the angel whose wings
grew on my either side, whose light
  flowed from my eyes,
or the quickness of my heart when I
  lifted up
to let what felt like a rush of cool air
  in,
and if I mention love and ascension,
or a lightness I have not felt
  in the past fifty years,
or the thought of joy, of streaming, of
  flying right there and then
through the opening into the mystery
  of the other side,
how could I even think of asking you
  to believe me,
since I did not go, since I stayed here
  with you instead.

The Ice-Cream Sandwich

In second grade I felt about him and
three other boys, quite equally, in a way
the Church identified, later, for me as lust.
He was short and square, chubby in the thigh,
with butter-colored hair. But none of this
explains why I put my vanilla ice-cream
sandwich in his pencil box which was
a work of art, its cardboard covered with green
paper stamped so that it looked like Mother's
tooled leather address book. Its little drawers
housed rows of pencils in all worldly colors.

My ice cream oozed through levels of his cardboard,
congealing pencils in its sweet pale soup,
and when the teacher, whose name I've forgotten,
asked, "Who did this?" I erupted
into tears, fled to the girls' room
and had to be scolded out of a locked stall
to run a gauntlet of giggles. Apologies
were futile. He knew I was crazy and kept
out of reach right through high school. Even now,
perhaps, there's a man, middle-aged in his
gray, three-piece suit, who suffers from
pencil-box trauma. What was I attempting
to say in blundering, fledgling symbolism?
You melt me? I want to melt you? Was I
a seven-year-old pencil-box fetishist
or an early case of role reversal?

I've never told an analyst about this, but
saved it all these years for you, who,
since you did that bizarre thing during nap time
or in the supply closet,
or under the hedge during recess, also
relive the inexplicable in middle age.

Sunday Morning Walk

Boise was my first city,
a place I imagined
at the end of a perilous
road of gravel slippery
as marbles, a road
with ravines on both sides
like the one in *The Thief
of Baghdad*. But going there
offered only Horseshoe Bend's
handful of butterflies.

Later the schoolyard was
dangerous with strangers
and the building
had too many rooms,
too many echoes
in the halls. And there were
sidewalks everywhere.
Once a yard fetishist
yelled at me for daring
to step on his lawn.
I hadn't noticed but
after that I made
a point of crossing it
every chance I got,
wishing only that my
feet were bigger,
my footprints deeper.

Our apartment was small
and dark as a cave, much
smaller than the house
back home I knew
was gone for good.
There was little work
in Boise which made

my parents talk late
as our savings went quarter
after quarter into the gas
meter. But on Sundays
we took walks and the days
were good—late fall
with its bluster
and knife edge and longing
for snow. That Sunday was
windy, too, and clear as we
walked toward the treat
of a restaurant breakfast.
Leaves blew and the big trees
complained like old stairs.
There was no traffic.
Far off as in a movie
we heard the Extra shouted.
Only that word in and out
of the wind but as we
got closer the words
defined themselves one
by one and by the time
we bought our paper
the war had started.

First

For me it was Robin Hentz:
in fourth grade *and* fifth grade she made me tense.

Her beauty was inexplicable and utterly cogent
like talent;
she reminded me of Prince Valiant.

Robin was quick and dark and small.
On our field trip to the planetarium, to be beside her
and have her see me
was the thing in the universe that mattered at all.

I don't know if she moved away
before I moved away (from Raleigh, NC),
somehow I don't recall;
but each of us needs a first discovery
of the kind of love into which you fall—
admiration maddening and immense—
and for me it was Robin Hentz.

First Kill

Love at eight is dust powdering the air,
a fine veil over white Keds after the slingshot
stone pushes a crater in, that thwack and sight
of an instant vanishing. You aimed at everything.
Cats wound away from stinging pebbles into shrubs.
Crows cawed, stepped into sky and back
to the branch like current.
        Now, doves slant
through the cloud-scarred dusk, apostrophes
owning the sag of wire and all its talk
between tarred poles dressing a road outside
a town too big to be a town anymore.
Mothers worry when the sun goes down,
when the fade of blue jeans blurs to night's first crease
between all this quiet and the hollering stars,
worry what you'll tell them, what you won't,
that you'd aimed at the sun through leaves and a blue jay
fell dead to the ground. Whoop it up, boy.
You hit the sky and it fell, plumb as you wanted.

Suzanne

This much I know, I walked through the scraggly wood
behind the Italian restaurant on the highway
south of Camden, my former girlfriend Joanne,
her sister, her white-haired mother, her niece Suzanne,
and we were waiting for dinner slow Suzanne and
I walked over the glass and the burning rubbish
downhill from the restaurant and when we came back
her mother was furious for it was dark and
disgusting out there and she was holding a lilac
she picked up from the fire and I was crestfallen,
the way I get, my neck was crimson, Suzanne
was smelling the burned lilac, she was seven.

First Time Going to School All by Myself

Barely light when I set off alone.
No sound but the chock of kicked rocks,
red steel lunch box clanking against my knee.
A half-mile walk in the near dark, my new shoes
slicking the narrow mud *isthmus* (my new word)
between two puddles trying to start a pond. Then past
the picked-over garden, and the scarecrow's milk-jug face
wouldn't look at me. Over the bridge of railroad ties
that spanned a stream-bed, snakes
who got to sleep late.

                    Looking back,
I could see through the fog
only the yellowish smear of the porch light.
Then the driveway took a turn,
putting even that out of sight.

It wasn't till then that I saw the webs,
whole fields choked with them,
no two weeds without one
drooping between. Big nets dripping from high
in the cedars, hundreds of single threads
stretched off to the field's end, over my head
or low in my path like tripwires. These couldn't be
spiders from earth.

                    I thought about turning back,
to warn my family, call the President,
tell him we were in for some hard times ahead.
If I acted quickly, I'd save us all.
But then I thought, no, let's wait
and see what happens. The school bus came,
blinking and bleeding red light into the fog,
and I climbed on.

What did I learn that day
about the world? Each morning the startling history
of spiders spells itself out in the dew
and once the sun's up—spy's ink—disappears.

What did I learn about myself? Was it fear
of looking foolish that stopped me that morning
from warning the world? No,
I kept a straight face, my mouth shut,
went to my seat, sat still,
stared out my window, rooted,
more than a little, for the monsters.

Hail

I was eleven the first time I saw it,
the November afternoon gone
heavy and gray. I'd begun
to doze when something—
not palm fronds rustling
nor monkey pods rattling,
but more like spoons against glass
or small bells—something began
clinking against the second story's
blue palings and rails, lightly at first,
bringing all of us, even the teacher,
to our feet and out the door.
                      Not since,
three years before, when the staticky
Standard Oil broadcast had been
interrupted by news that brought to tears
even Miss Engard (who didn't tax
our imaginations too hard playing
the part of witch at Halloween)
had there been so much commotion.
Seeing our teachers openly weeping
had frightened us even more than a word
like *assassination.*
               Above us,
concrete. Under our feet, concrete.
And all of us stretching our hands
beyond the blue rails to catch,
as they fell, clear pieces of sky
that burned a second,
melting in our hands.

for Betty Adcock

23

First Glasses

He told me what I could see twenty feet away
others could see clearly from eighty.
Driving home from downtown we took
the backroad studded with crabapples
my brother and I threw from the narrow height
of the school bus windows, my left hand
clutching the spelling bee word list:
McGee's Egg Stop, the cemetery, then
the quilted fields. There was never enough
to read in the afternoons—the *TV Guide*,
free magazines picked up in Tom Thumb
with listings for houses. Mother always
itched to move, and I loved boxing up
toys and records, fighting with my brother
for the biggest bedroom almost once a year.
I read phonebooks, dictionaries, and rummaged
the kitchen junk drawer where Mother kept
her greeting cards, their rhymes penned by no one,
almost personal in their printed cursive.
Even then I knew what was hand-written meant
more than the Hallmark script, although
Mother read each line regardless,
sometimes two or three times, needing
sentiment enough to read the words
as though they were truly the right ones,
the necessary, meant ones, as if
her heart could focus to fit the card.
Bedtime reading was the Bible
I'd open after dinner until my father found me
hours later, asleep. He'd pick the book up,
place it in my bed, say a Bible on the floor
was sacrilege. That year the local paper
pictured me in my new glasses,
with a headline that read, "SPELL 'SCOUNDREL'."
I lost the spelling bee by mistaking "scoundrel"
for "scandal," and spelled, I read that night,

"a publicized incident that brings about disgrace
or offends the moral sensibilities of society."
I didn't know, but I felt disgrace, a girl's
uncombed awkwardness, clumsy nightly navigations
down the hallway for water. Kids at school
called me Scoundrel for the few months we remained
and none of us knew what it meant
until I looked it up to find I was a villain,
a rogue, an unreliable person. The Old Testament
defined it "sinner," and I remember trembling
as Mother and I left the optometrist's office.
New-eyed, I saw each leaf, suddenly dangerous as a razor,
capable as any of us of drawing blood.

Frutas

Growing up in Miami any tropical fruit I ate
could only be a bad copy of the Real Fruit of Cuba.
Exile meant having to consume false food,
and knowing it in advance. With joy
my parents and grandmother would encounter
Florida—grown *mameyes* and *caimitos* at the market.
At home they would take them out of the American bag
and describe the taste that I and my older sister
would, in a few seconds, be privileged to experience
for the first time. We all sat around the table
to welcome into our lives this football-shaped,
brown fruit with the salmon-colored flesh
encircling an ebony seed. *"Mamey"*
my grandmother would say with a confirming nod,
as if repatriating a lost and ruined name.
Then she bent over the plate,
slipped a large slice of *mamey* into her mouth,
then straightened in her chair and, eyes shut,
lost herself in comparison and memory.
I waited for her face to return with a judgment.
"No, not even the shadow of the ones back home."
She kept eating, more calmly,
and I began tasting the sweet and creamy pulp
trying to raise the volume of its flavor
so that it might become a Cuban *mamey*. "The good
Cuban *mameyes* didn't have *primaveras*," she said
after the second large gulp, knocking her spoon
against a lump in the fruit and winking.
So at once I erased the lumps in my mental *mamey*.
I asked her how the word for "spring"
came to signify "lump" in a *mamey*. She shrugged.
"Next you'll want to know how we lost a country."

Peaches

In the only moment of ecstasy I have
with my mama, I see August
and her blue eyes float over wireless lenses
and two bushels of ripe peaches on the linoleum
ooze onto a stack of newspaper
foretelling more trouble in Vietnam.

She sits at the oak table on a maple chair
and pretends to talk
but she doesn't—can't—say much,
because she is staring at the peaches
and turning them, each one, pulling back skin,
opening Red Havens with quick twists,
and the knife is a minnow in and out
of golden pulp, funneling rot, flicking away fuzz
and her short fingers stream with juice.

The knife in my own hand is slippery,
jealous and sticky, and my face
is streaked with resin and peach fuzz
when I stop and watch.
What is it when a person holds a peach
with that urgency of touch, the slight trembling,
sliver of saliva at the corner of her mouth—

What did she think those peaches would do?
Was she going to send them to my brother
on his birthday to eat in a jungle, or raw
to put on bug bites, to suck out pus.
Would a peach a day keep the Cong away?

More than putting by, more
than the other side of the planet burning,
or knowing my brother was no more safe
than the peach from the knife,
it was the round, wet, short-lived seasons,

of small planets slipping through her narrow hands
that taught me.
She cut as a seduction,
as with the hunger of bloodlust,
a violence I had never before
watched or touched.

Foreplay

During recess in the fifth grade
giggling girls drew fat hearts
on the blackboard. They'd print
their names next to mine and shoot
arrows through them. My cheeks tinted
pink as I knelt on one knee, scaled
baseball cards against the back wall.
When I was twelve, we played "Hunter
and the Hunted" in couples. One team
counted, the other hid. Linda said no one
would find us and kissed my lips. She slipped
her tongue in my mouth, unzipped
my dungarees. I pinched her nipples,
listened for footsteps. High school,
I played lead guitar in a garage band.
We banged "Good Lovin" off gym walls
while tight skirt girls shimmied
near the amps. Cindy licked her lipstick,
threw me a kiss and yelled she'd wait for me.
In the back seat of her Dad's Rambler
she lifted her sweater, unsnapped
her bra. Anytime my fingers crept
up her leg, she pushed my hand away,
she'd say no, not tonight, not yet,
and press her knees together. Julia
was surprised when I said I never
made love before. We cut class
Wednesday morning, went to my empty house.
We locked the door, walked down basement
stairs. She sat on the edge of the bed.
I pulled down the shades. She stood up,
hugged me, then stepped back to undress.
When she caught me staring, I blushed.
She smiled, curled under blankets.
When I kissed the back of her neck,
she turned and opened her arms. All
of her skin touched all of mine.

Riding Lesson

Some days he lurched around
the ring, yelling in Irish. You circled him, he was
the sun, his name was Mick. With his long
whip, he cracked the indolence at your heels,
he made your spine sing its straightest song.

He was a drunk and cast a smelly shadow
while you sat soaping bridles in the tack room
where stirrups took the sun.
Your mother came at six, shafts of light
still hitting the roof of the Impala.

You stood on two hay bales and stared
as they paced in their stalls
wearing bright blankets stained with liniment.
A horse's breath formed a little
white cloud like a man's.

They had the same yellow teeth, the same
lathery sweat. You never knew
when they would turn. At Christmas
your father gave him a bottle, the paddock froze
and the water in the bathtub outside the barn.

After his car wreck, he sat in a plastic
chair and watched the lessons.
With his wet smile. His gimpy leg.
He snapped a crop, he cursed the air,
and then the city closed the stable.

He put the reins of a horse in your hands.
His laughter followed you and made you cry.
Crybaby! He was your first teacher.

Winged Snake Found on a Path

A long time ago, twelve hours from here
by car, on a small bit of acreage with a pond,
I was squatting in my shorts and contemplating
a poisoned, purple bean
when the grown-ups slapped it from my grasp.

It was hot in the air, in the furrows in the field.
It was cool on the black bottom of the pond,
and a chill rose from the deep
and settled under the trees.

I left the heat and circled the princely pond.
My head even then was too big,
and filled with trees.
And I almost did not see the winged snake
stretched across the path.
His long bright wings were battered and thin.
I knelt: someone had done him in.
And that was the last one I have seen.

The First One

Who knows what led me there—a twelve-year-old,
leading my eight-year-old brother and his overnight guest

into the one clean room of that four-story brownstone
and plunging into the booze while our parents slept.

Maybe it was genetic curiosity, colliding with vodka,
a fifth of cheap Russian, and scorching a freeway to our guts,

as we quivered on the oriental rug, passing the bottle
beneath the fancy paintings that held the walls up.

Consequence was a planet whose orbit we couldn't respect.
When the clear stuff got finished, red wine came next,

with little bits of the cork I wedged down with a knife
bobbing like chaperones forced to walk the plank.

The room began flipping like a pancake. We dropped
glass anchors from that third-story porthole,

transforming the neighbors into a frenzy of phone calls.
Who knows what emotions my parents were wearing,

but whatever they said didn't make any sense,
as we wiped our lips and spiraled into black.

Joining the Circus

Across the street, two large cottonwoods, a tree I've never
noticed since, named for the bits of fluff floating
near them. He was my best friend that summer,

and I was invited to stay for supper, across the street
at Ricky Johnson's, behind the cottonwoods and a rickety
garage, peeling white sides and a bungalow with front steps.

In the dark interior his father, a dark man,
and mother smoked cigarettes, or that's what made it
seem dark, as in a painting. His father, Stan,

ran the sporting goods store, where I had seen him
and watched a game of the World Series on the TV there.
At dinner we had bread with our food, white

bread and soft butter, half a loaf on a plate
for anyone to take. At home, so many miles
away, we have only the bread my mother has baked,

hard-crusted, never just waiting, in a stack,
and this is soft, luscious, white bread, my first time
renouncing the bright dining room of home forever.

Fingers in the Bread

Hardly the food revolt in "Potemkin"—
no bugs in the gruel or historic implications—
but the impulse to resist was surely the same
the day lunch consisted solely of soggy
corn fritters, Karo syrup, iceberg lettuce,
cream cheese balls dredged in peanut butter,
and piles of bread, squishy white loaves
dumped callously out of their wrappers.

I can't recall what made us all
start laughing instead of complaining
or leaving the tables; what made us
start throwing the cream cheese balls
at one another, until someone thought to
hurl them to the light bulbs and ceiling.

Then Sallie and I were drawn to the bread,
those stacked loaves, pushing our fingers
through the unresisting mush, laughing,
punching holes in all the loaves in the room,
schoolmates egging us on, and falling away,
noticing before we did—so absorbed
in our joy—teachers hurrying
from their own lunchrooms, with frowns.

Sallie had laughed as I couldn't remember
her laughing since her father died.
Good girls, top of our class, we shocked
everyone except the head teacher—
avuncular Miss White, who reminded us
of waste and world hunger, yet managed
to convey amusement, and even a kind
of approval. We were thirteen,
not sorry, though we pretended to be:
giddy from the first fight of our revolution.

Story of Sound

It begins in the vestry
with a customary two dollar bill
from groom to servers.
             My first wedding,
a scent of wine from cut glass cruets—
the same burgundy
color as the kneeler cushions
where they wait for their names
from the priest:
"Dominic Trancreda... Carmella Peronne...."

Her bridal veil is lifted,
a small yellow stain on the bodice,
the face pale,
a beauty mark above her parted lips...
"Do you, Carmella, take..."
Looking at me, she lowers her eyes
and the silence stretches to a yes.

That night, the newspaper says
her husband, a dent in the middle
of his heavy chin, is a butcher.
I clip her photo, carry her heart-
shaped face for months
behind the veil,
as if in a cocoon,
lips the color of a cherry
that tops the sundae
I'm famished for. Then, whispering
Carmella, Carmella,
I taste the sound
that deepens everything I see.

She wants
to live a certain kind of life
away from the block and cleaver,

the hateful apron smeared with red,
her voice urging,
Do it for me, Carmella,
that name in the night room turning
the barrel of a portrait lens—
Carmella at the altar of sleep
lovelier than any Madonna,
giving her name to my lips
even when awake.

Carmella.
I'm twelve,
married for the first time
to a name.

Horse

The first horse I ever saw
   was hauling a wagon stacked with furniture
      past storefronts along Knickerbocker Avenue.
He was taller than a car, blue-black with flies,

and bits of green ribbon tied to his mane
   bounced near his caked and rheumy eyes.
      I had seen horses in books before, but
this horse shimmered in the Brooklyn noon.

I could hear his hooves strike the tar,
   the colossal nostrils snort back the heat,
      and breathe his inexorable, dung-tinged fume.
Under the enormous belly, his——

swung like the policeman's nightstick,
   a dowsing rod, longer than my arm—
      even the Catholic girls could see it
hung there like a rubber spigot.

When he let loose, the steaming street
   flowed with frothy, spattering urine.
      And when he stopped to let the junkman
toss a tabletop onto the wagon bed,

I worked behind his triangular head
   to touch his foreleg above the knee,
      the muscle jerking the mat of hair.
Horse, I remember thinking,

four years old and standing there,
   struck momentarily dumb,
      while the power gathered in his thigh
surged like language into my thumb.

Fowler Street

Danny Drolet
told me.
"I caught my big
brother in the garage
looking at a book
filled with dirty
pictures. He blew
two smoke rings, pointed
his cigarette between
this girl's legs," said
"That's where you stick
your dick." I didn't
believe him.

We were standing
on the corner
throwing snowballs
at cars crawling
along Fowler street.
I threw one
through an open
bus window, hit
the driver and knocked
his glasses off.
When he slowed
to a stop, we hopped
a backyard fence, tore
ass down the alley.
Out of breath
he crossed his heart
swore it was true.

I didn't say
a word, thought
I'd be late for supper
and ran all the way.

I sat down, bowed
my head and said
grace, watched Mom
pass serving dishes, Dad
spoon goulash, Julie
chew egg noodles
with her mouth
open, and I knew
it was true.

Learning to Swim at Poverty Beach

A few yards out the drop
dropped fifty feet into darkness
dredged for submarines and spider crabs
whose intricate webs, I imagined,
would wrap around my feet
and pull me under.
At night on the damp sand older boys
laid down their girls who let them
go deep, coming up weak, soggy,
and out of breath.

This was years before I realized
how stupid I was, and lucky.
Years before the draft board leveled
the neighborhood, before Walter Wetzel
took his famous last jump shot,
before Becker and O'Leary and Roe
and San Fillipo doped themselves
into graves so shallow, I swear I saw them
shooting up again on Cross Bay Boulevard.
This was years before I noticed
how car lights crossing Jamaica Bay
could turn the dark, dirty water
into something almost beautiful.

Treasure

Ax heads and sledges, musket balls and elixir bottles,
the earth cleans its room without having to be told;
as if putting tools back neatly into the case of the ground,
history knows precisely where each of us goes.

This is close to what the boy must think, he who already
has a boy buried inside him, who, like a nine-volt battery,
can be removed and handled. His head is a bottle cap,
his torso a wound mass of baling wire. And when the boy
holds this small self he can sit ringed with mushrooms
on the decaying stump of his father's childhood
and feel every turn the earth makes
driving home through the dark.

He has excavated an entire vacation. He has passed this wand
over miles of pull-tabs and coffee cans teeming with grubs and beetles.
But this is his first unearthing of unadulterated sorrow,
of all he cannot remember, or forget, or undo.

He is only ten. The metal detector, which now lies
chirping across his knees, is destined for his dim closet.
But it has found him and that was worth everything.
And now that he has found himself,
these glances of light, the uncouplings
of birdsong, of leaf from leaves,
what if he were to step forward into that future,
his heart thudding like a thermos in a lunch pail,
what if he were to rise like mist from the forest floor
then turn from the flint-nicked trowel of the season?

He sees it is like those grainy silent comedies
in which someone is asked to volunteer,
then the entire cast but one steps back.
Someone has to do it. Someone has to be the past
with its drawn, saddened, weary face,
someone has to be the bullet-pocked backdrop,

that retaining wall of shame and wailing,
the collector of evidence
against which all else is measured.

The Picnic

It is the picnic with Ruth in the spring.
Ruth was third on my list of seven girls
But the first two were gone (Betty) or else
Had someone (Ellen has accepted Doug).
Indian Gully the last day of school;
Girls make the lunches for the boys too.
I wrote a note to Ruth in algebra class
Day before the test. She smiled, and nodded.
We left the cars and walked through the young corn
The shoots green as paint and the leaves like tongues
Trembling. Beyond the fence where we stood
Some wild strawberry flowered by an elm tree
And Jack-in-the-pulpit was olive ripe.
A blackbird fled as I crossed, and showed
A spot of gold or red under its quick wing.
I held the wire for Ruth and watched the whip
Of her long, striped skirt as she followed.
Three freckles blossomed on her thin, white back
Underneath the loop where the blouse buttoned.
We went for our lunch away from the rest,
Stretched in the new grass, our heads close
Over unknown things wrapped up in wax papers.
Ruth tried for the same, I forget what it was,
And our hands were together. She laughed,
And a breeze caught the edge of her little
Collar and the edge of her brown, loose hair
That touched my cheek. I turned my face in—
to the gentle fall. I saw how sweet it smelled.
She didn't move her head or take her hand.
I felt a soft caving in my stomach
As at the top of the highest slide
When I had been a child, but was not afraid,
And did not know why my eyes moved with wet
As I brushed her cheek with my lips and brushed
Her lips with my own
lips. She said to me

Jack, Jack, different than I had ever heard,
Because she wasn't calling me, I think,
Or telling me. She used my name to
Talk in another way I wanted to know.
She laughed again and then she took her hand;
I gave her what we both had touched—can't
Remember what it was, and we ate the lunch.
Afterward we walked in the small, cool creek
Our shoes off, her skirt hitched, and she smiling:
My pants rolled, and then we climbed up the high
Side of Indian Gully and looked
Where we had been, our hands together again.
It was then some bright thing came in my eyes,
Starting at the back of them and flowing
Suddenly through my head and down my arms
And stomach and my bare legs that seemed not
To stop in feet, not to feel the red earth
Of the Gully, as though we hung in a
Touch of birds. There was a word in my throat
With the feeling and I knew the first time
What it meant and I said, it's beautiful.
Yes, she said, and I felt the sound and word
In my hand join the sound and word in hers
As in one name said, or in one cupped hand.
We put back on our shoes and socks and we
Sat in the grass awhile crosslegged, under
A blowing tree, not saying anything.
And Ruth played with shells she found in the creek,
As I watched. Her small wrist which was so sweet
To me turned by her breast and the shells dropped
Green, white, blue, easily into her lap,
Passing light through themselves.
She gave the pale
Shells to me, and got up and touched her hips
With her light hands, and we walked down slowly
To play the school games with the others.

First Love, Sixteen Years Old

The river through the dirty mill town
Trills, descants, murmurs, and blabs.

A face considers a mirror.
A handsome cloud stares back.

In the early morning
The dark, funky scent of evening.

Hand in hand,
Fingers eager as birds.

The personal frequencies of taste:
Each rock band an avowal.

To smile benignly at parents
And the ancient silt of their habits.

In the unfrequented park, fountains
Jetting rhapsodies: "You know me."

Looking back down a street at someone
Looking back down a street.

A diary in a backpack—
The smudged quiver of lyric.

The Cry

Then, everything slept.
The sky & the fields slept all the way to the Pacific,
And the houses slept.
The orchards blackened in their sleep,
And, outside my window, the aging Palomino slept
Standing up in the moonlight, with one rear hoof slightly cocked,
And the moonlight slept.
The white dust slept between the rows of vines,
And the quail slept perfectly, like untouched triangles.
The hawk slept alone, apart from this world.
In the distance I could see the faint glow
Of Parlier—even its name a lullaby,
Where the little bars slept with only one light on,
And the prostitutes slept, as always,
With the small-time businessmen, their hair smelling of pomade,
Who did not dream.
Dice slept in the hands of the town's one gambler, & outside
His window, the brown grass slept,
And beyond that, in a low stand of trees, ashes slept
Where men with no money had built a fire, and lain down,
Beside the river,
And saw in their sleep how the cold shape of fire
Made, from each crystal of ash, the gray morning,
Which consoled no one.
Beside me, my brother slept
With a small frown knitted into his face, as if
He listened for something, his mouth open.
But there was nothing.
On my last night as a child, that sleep was final.
Above me, the shingles slept on the roof,
And the brick chimney, with smoke rising through it, slept,
And the notes on sheet music slept.
I went downstairs, then, to the room
Where my mother & father slept with nothing on, & the pale light
Shone through the window on the candor
Of their bodies strewn over the sheets, & those bodies

Were not beautiful, like distant cities.
They were real bodies
With bruises & lattices of fatigue over their white stomachs,
And over their faces.
His hair was black, & thinning. Hers was the color of ashes.
I could see every detail that disappointment had sketched,
Idly, into them: her breasts & the widening thigh
That mocked my mother with the intricate,
Sorrowing spasm of birth;
I could see
The stooped shoulders & sunken chest of my father,
Sullen as the shape of a hawk in wet weather,
The same shape it takes in its death,
When you hold it in your outstretched hand,
And wonder how it can shrink to so small a thing,
And then you are almost afraid, judging by the truculence
Of its beak & the vast, intricate plan
Of its color & delicate shading, black & red & white,
That it is only sleeping,
Only pretending a death.
But both of them really unlike anything else
Unless you thought, as I did,
Of the shape of beaten snow, & absence, & a sleep
Without laughter.
They lay there on their bed.
I saw every detail, & as I turned away
Those bodies moved slightly in the languor of sleep,
And my mother cried out once, but did not awaken,
And that cry stayed on in the air—
And even as I turned away, their frail bodies,
Seen as if for a last time,
Reminded me of ravines on either side of the road,
When I ran,
And did not know why.

TWO

First Kiss

Her mouth
fell into my mouth
like a summer snow, like a
5th season, like a fresh Eden,

like Eden when Eve made God
whimper with the liquid
tilt of her hips—

her kiss   hurt like that—
I mean, it was as if she'd mixed
the sweat of an angel
with the taste of a tangerine,
I swear! My mouth

had been a helmet forever
greased with secrets, my mouth—
a dead-end street a little bit
lit by teeth—my heart, a clam
slammed shut at the bottom of a dark,

but her mouth pulled up
like a baby-blue Cadillac
packed with canaries driven
by a toucan—I swear

those lips said bright
wings when we kissed, wild
and precise—as if she were
teaching a seahorse to speak—
her mouth   so careful, chumming
the first vowel from my throat

until my brain was a piano
banged loud, hammered like that—
it was like, I swear   her tongue

was Saturn's 7th moon—
hot like that, hot
and cold and circling,

circling, turning me
into a glad planet—
sun on one side, night pouring
her slow hand over the other: one fire

spooning the lake of another.
Her kiss, I swear—if
the Great Mother rushed open
the moon like a gift and you
were there to feel your shadow
finally unhooked from your wrist:

that'd be it but even sweeter—
like a riot of one-legged priests
on pogo-sticks, up and up,
this way   and *this*, not
falling but on and on
like that, badly behaved
but holy—I swear! That

kiss, both lips utterly committed
to the world   like a Peace Corps,
like a free store, forever and always
a new city—no locks, no walls, just
doors—like that, I swear,
like that.

First Kiss

Afterwards you had that drunk, drugged look
my daughter used to get, when she had let go
of my nipple, her mouth gone slack and her eyes
turned vague and filmy, as though behind them
the milk was rising up to fill her
whole head, that would loll on the small
white stalk of her neck so I would have to hold her
closer, amazed at the sheer power
of satiety, which was nothing like the needing
to be fed, the wild flailing and crying until she fastened
herself to me and made the seal tight
between us, and sucked, drawing the liquid down and
out of my body; no, *this* was the crowning
moment, this giving of herself, knowing
she could show me how helpless
she was—that's what I saw, that night when you
pulled your mouth from mine and
leaned back against a chain link fence,
in front of a burned-out church: a man
who was going to be that vulnerable,
that easy and impossible to hurt.

Fall

It was a wing, it was a kiss,
soft as a word, or as breath
in the middle of a word, it moved
through the air like smoke then fell
as quietly and deliberately
as any falling thing, a word,
a wing, a leaf, or sunlight
falling through leaves, heavier
than air, the way music
falls sometimes, or wind
after a storm has cleared
But it was softer than that,
really, like new snow falling
on the still-green grass by the side
of the road, or a certain kind of silence
I thought I saw clouds in the distance,
I thought I saw an olive tree,
or a birch, maybe
I thought there was wind
and branches moving overhead
and the birds knew me
It was a wing, a word, a blade, a kiss
It was a song, it was a kind of singing
as if somewhere someone was singing
and I could hear the air moving
through it, that perfect rushing sound
like blood rushing over bone
But it was more than breath, more than
music really, the vestige of some
elemental language suspended
in space, then falling the way a leaf
falls, or a voice, any voice
I thought it called out to me
I thought it said my name
in the pure reverence of light
and air, right where I stood,

the rain sinking its small
bright teeth into the earth
But it wasn't rain, it was not
that kind of falling, not
rain, not a stone, never a stone
though I could feel the weight of it
the way a stone has weight
and texture, and language, and a voice
And if I leaned my ear against
the trembling mouth of it
I could hear my own name softly
falling, a shining, falling thing
like a coin or a wish,
it was that real, it was
in the air, it was still falling

Sequence

First
    Standing in her basement
    pressing her

    against a door
    all the years

    of anticipation
    beating their wings

    inside me
    before she could

    show me
    what to do

Second
    She kissed
    what had never
    been kissed

    And I could
    only kiss
    her back

Third
    We drove around
    looking
    for a place
    to park

    until we turned
    that corner
    and found
    a lot

with many
empty spaces
each needing
to be filled

First Drink

Valerie and I were only going to take a sip
from the bottle of tequila Jeff Hudson
had stolen from the Piersons' garage
and hidden behind the bleachers, just one
little swig for two little tipplers
sitting on a bench, dressed for the dance,
bows in our hair, the green pool of the football field
shimmering in the sun still high
in the sky as I slammed my first taste back
which came right back up, but I wanted to know
the alchemy of alcohol, the lushness of liquor,
the buzz of booze, wanted to get drunk as a skunk,
plastered and hammered, tanked and stewed,
trashed and sloshed, bombed and blitzed,
sozzled and soused, pie-eyed and plowed,
it was my birthright, my bloodline, my DNA,
so with the strength of generations, I kept it down.
I said to my friend, "Let's have another,"
and we passed the bottle around until
the field was drained and the sun went blind,
the worm turned white and the seraphs arrived,
each with three pairs of wings, then four then five,
swinging and singing and flying
us so far out of our minds our bodies levitated
and finally landed in our respective backyards.
I lay on a chaise lounge, bow tilted, head toppled
toward the vomit while Mother yelled,
Who the hell did this? And I didn't say
I did it myself, it was awfully fun.
The next day I stood at the fridge
with an unquenchable thirst,
I would do it again,
I would have another and another,
I had not learned my lesson,
it had just begun.

First Time at the Wheel

Sunlight one Sunday afternoon, and dust
on the bumpy road through Marstson's field
which lay on the banks of the river between
the water and the hump of Indian Ridge—
the three of us and Mr. Burrows, ex-GI,
who bore a stitch of scars around his middle
where bullets were machine-gunned
in, but he survived to teach us
how to drive in his converted jeep rollbarred
for the worst, in case we caromed off
through furrows bristling with desiccated corn
or slammed into boles of oaks along the river.
We cranked the clutch and yanked
the shiftstick, then bucked ahead
to swerve across a washboard of exposed roots
until we found a little turnspot at the end,
carved out of sumac, and careened around it,
hooting, terrified but happy, while he bellowed
Shift it down, god damn it, shift it down!
We shredded metal, jammed the brakes
and hurtled forward, trying to coordinate our feet,
a little dance of easy-does-it, a little waltz
around a weed-choked road that led
to keep-on-going, pour-it-on-and-don't-look-back.

Ooh My Soul
—*Little Richard*

By night, ghosts roam Aunt Ermyn's
elm-shrouded, hundred-year-old home.
By day, my cousin Pete, just out of high school
combs his duck-tail and keeps time
to records with his creaky rocking chair.
I'm in the hall, creating all-star teams
of baseball cards when, blaring
through Pete's open door, I hear...
war-drums? Or is it a runaway train?
A colored preacher shrieks,
Keepa knockin' but you cain't come in,
then squeals like tires around a curve.
Those chugging drums, smoking piano,
squawking duck-call saxophones
make me feel like an oil rig ready to blow.
I see wells pumping, teeter-totters bumping,
giant turtle-heads working out and in
as bronco riders wave tall hats in the air.
I see girls twirling, dresses swirling
high over their underwear,
guys doing splits, or inch-worming
across the floor.
                    It makes me want
to slam my head back and forth
like a paddle ball—to jump, shout, bang
my hands on walls, and flap them
in the air—to fall onto the ground
and writhe, flail, roar like Johnny Cerna
in his famous Kiddieland tantrum.
Keepa knockin' but you cain't come in,
the preacher howls. But I am in.
I'm in the living room, Bandstand on TV,
Dad ranting, "Goddamn Congo Beat!"
I'm in the back seat of his Ford

a decade later, learning what that beat
could be. I'm in my first band, hoarse
from screaming *Long Tall Sally.*
I'm in my college dorm, trying to jam
that wild abandon into poems.
I'm in my car, heading for work
when *Good Golly, Miss Molly!*
catapults out of my Blaupunkt stereo.
I'm walking into Pete's bedroom,
where I've never dared to go. *Oh,*
womp bompalumomp, a lomp bam boom!
I'm not thinking in words, but I know
I've spent my seven years rehearsing
how to feel this way. It's more exciting
than a touchdown any day, or a home run,
a gunfight, hurricane waves at Galveston,
a five-pound bass on a cane pole.
"What is that?" I ask Pete. He says,
"Rock and roll."

Orphic Night

I felt the absence of perspective—
Light shimmering above me, filtered

Through moving water; the path
Glistening, wet, grass blades
Flickering between the stones.

I felt certain of everything
Behind me: memory

Like the river's surface,
Flat, reflecting back

My face, the willows
Shifting in the breeze. I felt

Myself drawn forward,
Footsteps on marshy ground.
Clouds opening as if the sky, opaque,

Then clear, confused
What was about to happen with
A memory, the surface

Seen from underneath: dark shapes, a hull,
The moon refracted double as it rose.

Pried open, green, a pair of eyes
That watched me as I watched
Myself—it was not

Longing but the need
To look away: I turned

To you, already
Receding, restoring

The distance, and I knew
We'd be lovers forever.

The Widening

At the crucial moment she said yes. His hand in the back pocket of her jeans had made her wet—but nothing and no one had prepared her. They were on her bed, at boarding school. Naked she was self-conscious, and self-conscious she was timid. He would know what to do if only she let him. He dug in, snapping her awake. She remembered letting herself be kissed when she was twelve, pulled into the bushes by a classmate, happily ambushed, titillated, but sure right up until the moment his lips pressed hers that she would not be kissed, no matter how long they sat nested together in the shrubs, because it was forbidden. She knew she could not bear it if she conceived, and she said no, pushing his shoulders hard with her hands. At once he was off, up, and out the door. Why had he left? In the bathroom, she looked and saw what she'd heard she'd find: blood. Her body pounded and throbbed, with the widening had come a great unremitting pressure on her bones and she ached inside. And that was it, she'd lost something she'd not examined having, something that until then had seemed irrelevant, illusory.

First Blow-Job

Suddenly I knew how it was to be my uncle's Labrador retriever,
young pup paddling furiously back across the pond with the prize
duck in her mouth, doing the best she could to keep her nose in the air

so she could breathe. She was learning not to bite, to hold the duck
just firmly enough, to command its slick length without leaving marks.
She was about to discover that if she reached the shore, delivered this

duck just the way she'd been trained, then Master would pet her
head and make those cooing sounds, maybe later he'd let her ride
in the cab of the truck. She would rest her chin on his thigh all the way

home, and if she'd been good enough, she might get to wear
the rhinestone-studded collar, he might give her a cookie, he might
not shove her off the bed when he was tired and it was time to sleep.

Development

I learned to fuck one summer in a burgeoning subdivision.
Half-finished houses belted my neighborhood's swelling paunch
and inside them, on unfinished floors, under dusty light from windows
still manufacturer-stickered, I acted play-husband to
                                        Nicky DeBoer's play-wife.
These were the booming early eighties, and once a house's roof was up,
we had maybe three days of unwedded bliss before the appliances came,
and with them the locksmiths. By summer's end I had to pedal for miles
to reach what we called "the starts," Nicky in front on my bike's banana seat,
steering while my thighs windmilled against her hips. We rode past homes
that had once been ours, now occupied, lost behind swarms
                                        of marigolds and toddlers.
In some we had passed milestones—first French kiss, first finger—
and as we blew past these Nicky turned to me and winked.
One day was to be like none before: I'd filched a Trojan
and we'd staked out a just-roofed ranch with an unlocked patio door.
As I pedaled out to the development's limit, tingling with lust,
an ambulance screamed past us toward the center, where split-levels
built in the fifties housed the recently retired. And later, afterward,
cracking up at the thought that this ludicrous, stunted thing was
what all the fuss was about, we saw that ambulance drive back out: slowly,
unlighted, bumping along the unpaved road in a dusty cloak of progress.

Fifteen

Late that summer my girlfriend's boyfriend
came home from a year in the Merchant Marine
blond and tanned and drove her away
in his cut-down souped-up '36 Ford.
On the swinging sofa in her backyard
my hand had been drawn down her dress, and she
had straightaway promised that henceforth we
were nearly married and never would part.
Now she was parked on a hill above town
with that tattooed bastard and I had no car.

I'd blow him sky high with a match in his tank,
I promised and walked to her house. In the hedge,
doubled up, I waited half the night
with her purring cat that lifted its chin
to be scratched. The cat was all I had left.
Then, with the radio blaring "Moonlight and Roses",
they coasted up, both in the driver's seat.
I crouched while her mother blinked the porch light,
and my lost Nancy jumped out of the car,
skipped up to her door, and the cat ran in.

The little twin taillights disappeared down the street,
and the house went dark. What should I do?
I backed carefully out of the hedge,
ducked to the sidewalk, and sank my fists
deep in my pockets. Where could I walk
but home? And whom could I tell how the moon,
who had been featured in my songs
until I thought he rhymed with love,
was a yellow sphere with some blue shadows,
above the trees, moving across the sky?

4-H

1.
Four big Zimmerman farm boys rounded
a metal enameled table. The biggest one

red-faced and pudgy-fingered, a vicious Santa,
slammed a claw hammer calling order to the meeting.

The members munched up platters of cheddar
and summer sausage while winter howled

like a Holstein out of hell or hell-raising
farm boys drunk on too much home-brew.

2.
At Theresa, as usual, the older members met
while we played outside in the summer evening's

schoolyard full of fireflies and mosquitoes—
until I ran head first, pell-mell into

the metal monkey bars. I landed flat
on my back, and James, my best friend,

split a gut, "Ha ha ha!"
Or was he calling out for help?

3.
You can outlive getting kicked by a cow.
James's brother had to get metal plates in his head

because the silo crank came back and walloped him.
You'd think it would've killed him, but it didn't.

Even dad got it full in the head with a baseball bat
while playing catcher at school. He just lay on the couch

unconscious for hours and went out to milk the cows
the next morning. Of course, there was a slew that didn't make it,

like the Wilson kid killed by a car, but most
were only in farm accident videos.

4.

Then I was old enough, and it was my turn
to man the 7UP food stand at the county fair

and give presentations on different breeds
of goats: Nubian, LaMancha, Toggenburg

and Alpine, like the one I trimmed and deloused
and won a white ribbon on, even though I wept

like a baby about something not related to goats
or goat presentation, like the time dad left me

watching the cow show and I found myself
holding the strange man's hand.

The Single Urge

Peggy Everett, my first girlfriend, explains
That she is not so much leaving me as going
To someone else. I look at her as if
She were a mountain peak in the next county.
Later, I try to educate the mirror in my room
But the mirror is not interested. It is only me
On a certain day, short in stature and short on knowledge,
Keen on the brazen inconsequence of desire.

I stay up late and try to imagine what it
Is like to be in her body. How can pleasure be
Confused? We had agreed and I still agree
With the single urge that looks out windows, writes
Names in the margins of notebooks and is always
Ready to merge with what it lacks, what it believes.

The Eclipse
for my lover, on her birthday

Having never been to a drive-in movie
I can only imagine the god-size

of the owl's shadow across the screen,
the great bird soaring in front of the projector,

obliterating hugely with a slow swoop
what had been a comedy

and promised to have a car chase.
Every person in every car

like a cherry in a bon-bon.
How the soundtrack seemed to hold its breath:

out of the light, over there,
something smaller was sure to die.

The popcorn held its breath;
the rows of marooned cars

rusted deliberately in the sea air,
everyone's evening eclipsed by the owl.

Such ferocious majesty,
the bird of prey immense, wing-tips

feathered with cinematic light—
in the moment you look up from a first kiss

with the boy who will be your first lover.
It was June or July, you are sure.

What film? Who could remember.
All anyone who was there could want

is to be filled again
with the owl's shadow.

The cars nose home.
A teenager in the back seat,

you turn to the passenger-side window
where the stars beat against the glass.

All the Pools in Queens

Joey, the head lifeguard,
is the first to hire you for your looks.
The unpaid days it rains
you sit in your tin-can car, water
tapping the roof like fingernails.
He lights a fat blunt to share. The wipers
smudge and fog you in. His lips loom large,
rubbery. You want your underpaid job.

Nights, restless kids scale the pool's fence,
sink all the patio furniture in the deep end.
You're out driving barefoot,
looking for anyone else.

Mornings, you dive for lounge chairs,
ferry weighted umbrellas upwards.
Holding your breath—long like that—
makes your heart jump. Men

in black socks, sandals, tiny speedo suits,
wink. Women tip you a buck
to set up card tables for canasta.

In the heat people slump and fuse
like glass, edges rounding, topography
melting for good. The ex-cons in for free swim—
sex offenders at the local halfway house—
pretend to drown. One with an Elvis mullet
cops your phone number from the guard list
tacked to the shack wall. Your father
hangs up on him for weeks—

blames you. But you're eating
warm sandwiches, cleaning stubbed toes,
yelling at deck-runners, whistle-twirling

and smacking yourself in the thigh,
counting heads disappearing
below the surface.

Trade Show

First time in a sales booth
with my father,
I watched him hold a woman's torso in his hand,
then raise her overhead,
and slam her
into a wall, breasts first.
I heard the acrylic body thud
but when he held her up,
there wasn't a scratch on her, no crack, no mark
and the buyers went wild.

Men in suits lined up to take a turn.
Some threw her
against the fire door; others
ground their heels into her chest,
but couldn't break her breasts, a perfect 34.
Father showed them how
a (patent pending) plate, printed with their logo,
snapped into the base, how *Magicform*
would display their wares, their name.

I loved the way he smiled at me
when I smashed two *Magicforms* together,
when I dared the toughest-looking men
to beat them with their fists,
joking with the buyers
about my girlfriend's tits
being hard like these.
I felt the sweat, the heady spin
underneath the lights, the rush of adrenaline
earning my place
in the company of men.

The First Time I Heard Elvis

My father was on the tractor up ahead,
Danny and Gary and Billy and me
crowded in the truck cab behind,
chaff down our backs. Billy
and me had set fire to a haystack the week before,
and damn near caught the barn, and we'd
just gotten past that trouble. Truck radio suddenly
played we were nothing
but hound dogs. Chaff down our backs,
and Billy and me really did set a dangerous fire,
if anybody was a hound
dog it was us. Gary and Danny knew better than do
a fool thing like that. But listen,
now listen to this guy, what's his name,
Preston or something? Billy and me,
scratching our backs, looking
at Dad up ahead who can't hear it, this
loose-lipped tune, the first I ever knew him not hearing something.
And shit, just think all the heartbreak to come,
all the uncaught rabbits,
and Gary going for a life on the road, and Billy
in Pendleton as you might have supposed. Just hounds
like the rest of us. Not high class. No sir.

My Father's First Fight

Coated with blood, he canters home
waving his blue fists in victory.

His siblings want to sponge his knee,
lay a steak on his eye, call Dr. Gianni
to suture the cut on his cheek.

But he needs his father to see him
like some bloated big-time boxer
who made the other guy look worse.

Only eleven, he brags his opponent was fifteen.
His mother enters; hands and hair full of flour.
She collapses in mist into a chair.

One of his sisters fans her
using the newspaper, the dog barks
at the fresh scab on the tip of her brother's ear.

Wiping his brow with her apron,
his mother fusses for a towel
but he leaps from her fingers
shouting Papa! Papa! And from the belly

of his study his father puts down his bills,
steps to the stairwell and frowns
at his baby's swollen features.

He waves his whole arm in a backhand gesture
that turns his body away
from his youngest son.

At the closed door, the women
resume their hovering, sponging,
cooing, the flutter of care—

a weepy blur to the warrior
robbed of his honor.

The Doe

What does it matter
what I was thinking
when I aimed at a quivering branch
and braced my whole body
for the kick of that Browning 4.10?

All I could do was watch
the wet-velvet leg of something alive
sliding from the spattered white haunches
of the thing that lay dead on the snow.
All I could do was wait

while my father laid a hand on her belly,
unsnapped the strap
of the scabbard that hung from his belt,
then opened her pelt with a jerk:
as a steaming blue hose spilled out,

a sopping pouch like a red jellyfish,
and a leathery knot that he worked
out of the ribs in his fist—
lifting his big hands from the carcass
and smearing his cheeks till they shined.

All I could feel was the sticky stripe
burning when he touched my forehead,
his rough fingers making
what I knew, even then, was a sign:
of manhood, of *forgiveness*, I thought

until the wet fawn at our feet
shivered and opened its eyes,
until I saw him thumb a green shell
into his rifle, then slide
the oily bolt home.

The Hunt

To be in the way, belonging. To wait
Until paths cross. The aspen do not know,
Despite what you heard or imagined

Before dawn. The idea: to be still
As stone. To enter the stand and not move
Until she finds you, to be darkness

And then light breaking in. One of you
Will make a mistake. And what happens remains
In a tree others walk by on their way to water
Or desire or perhaps to die, and even if you leave

With the ringing still in your ears,
Even if she is no longer wanted,
She enters you like a forgotten road;
She makes a bed on your tongue and lies down.

Into First

Sixteen to the day, the first time
I legally sat in that front left seat.
Gripping the wheel—the roundness
of the world waiting—a hot black ribbon
laid below me, promising escape.
A fire-red Pinto, that defective
Detroit masterpiece famous
for exploding when rear-ended,
was mine, bought by countless
busboy dishes, and now, probably
compressed smaller than a mattress.
On my right for a change, my father
trying not to shout, ready to ride out
motion sickness, waited for me to find
the dual-foot, heel-toe sweet spot
combination. I eased out the clutch,
feeling for the right amount
of footpound push and release.
Then, the shudders,
the hesitation as she begged fuel
while commanded forward. Our
heads, practicing for whiplash,
rattled like insects in an epileptic
kid's jar. I restarted, tried again,
the stick forward into first,
the sweat-wet wheel and AM
radio all under my shaky sway.
That black ribbon and everywhere it
could take us waited, and behind,
an ugly childhood of inertia I left
as I slid the stick into second.
My father beside me tried to encourage,
not puke, his knuckles regaining color
as he watched me go.

Orientation: Wittenberg University, 1983

A mock class. My mother and I
are the only faces of color.
I've never studied with white people,
but I've had my experiences.
And sometimes having experience
is the only way to study people.
But what is the name for this color
the body turns when out of place? I

can see that I'm not ready.
The class is titled The Fall
and After, which is a study
of what happens after innocence, it's loss.
At this point, I understand loss
more than what comes before. A study
lending itself more to the act of falling,
an art in itself: How to appear ready

to step into the next stanza of life,
while tumbling down a page.
But, for now, in this classroom, the discussion
of Gauguin, Blake and the bible
passes over our heads. Suddenly the bible
is a foreign text. In the way they're discussing
it. I look down at the page
and it looks as blank as the life

I must have lived up to this moment.
The new students and the parents
are getting into this lecture, talking
about the art of falling. No hard times
or unfaithful lovers come up; this time
the blues can't frame the talk.
It's clear that, for some, life is a parent's
attempt to prepare a child for this moment:

When you walk into a room full of the educated
and you need to know what the hell
is going on. After class, my mother turns to me,
and says "You know, you don't..." she pauses,
"You don't have to do this," which gives me pause;
she's never said anything like this to me
before. I know without skills any job is hell,
but then you begin your education.
I decide what to do before she even gives me an out,
while we sit here, on the verge of knowing,
surrounded by people who sound like they know—
me with a Jheri curl, she in a wig—setting out
to make a mockery of class, my mother and I.

THREE

Firsts in No Particular Order

Purple towel on Grove, down comforter on South Davenport,
deck in Lonelyville, then of course—that rug burn at John's—

A Buddhist Temple storage closet over the humid dojo—

Squid

My mother in a pine coffin on a late morning in early March
before they slid her body in the furnace for all time—

"Ruby Tuesday" on the car radio before the caesarean; "Louie
Louie" before the vaginal-

Grandpa's teeth in a glass and shame, shame for laughing—

White moire tafetta. Snow. The Police.

Pinky

Air Pocket

The Waldorf-Astoria

Levine's "Gin"

Dialectical historical materialism, lumpen proletariat,
dictatorship of the proletariat, moribund capitalism,—

Olivetti Lettera 22—

Keep her cool. It's a fevral seizure. Not uncommon.

Chlorine

The lights opened on my powdered white face, tiny red lips and
skeins of pink silk—a dance my daughters will dance—

K-I-M   M-O-M

Eight hundred quarters—

My mother, my mother—

Rowing with daddy in the Catskills even while it poured—

Martini up with olives—was it stirred?

New Year

Let me dive to the bottom of the hotel pool

And find my mother's hairpin. Let me sit
With the mouth of a drowning woman on my lap

And add my breath to hers. In the dark,

Let me lay the thin white sheet of moon-light
Over the blue plums of my lover's breasts.

With the new planet I discovered just

When I thought I was losing my sight,
With the sun running down my chin,

Let me love another man because I will

Be a woman. Everything important will never
As yet have happened. Let it happen.

Let me throw a lit match on the secrets

My body has kept from me and stand
In the fire. Let the people I have sawed in half

Appear in my mirror, getting dressed.

Thank You for Being You

Poetry begins here. Brand new summer
faces the academy of youth. Gold
division buys gold. Everybody grew up
in a subculture, overcoming presentation.
Explosive subjectivity, anxiety loops,
available light digging Manhattan.
When things sound alike, does it
make them sisters? Come dancing
bitter city, it's only natural.
Carousel with its horses removed,
suddenly I don't feel so abandoned.
I want to communicate with you,
I'm trying as hard as a human,
but the white space always stops
me. When they found him he was
holding a shovel. When I loved
you all afternoon, you were absent,
the neighbors woken, your cries
were the actual miracle. Neither
heartbreaking nor a work
of genius staggered
by a little square of circumstance
is your skin. Defeated, I tell
endless bedtime stories, bounce
off others, understand power.
Even feedback can be helpful. Move
the radio to a slightly bigger
basement where it won't be too proud.
Restless spirit, it's you. You
are family, you are dark mysterious
helpful time for time to pull
in a little, curl up with some reasons,
and shut out the world.

The Sphere

Their first time, they were wonderfully tender
toward one another, so tenderness moved
still deeper into the core of each. A cottage

bed, mattress over a plywood platform nailed
to thick log legs. Torn patchwork quilt.
Near the window with a dozen small panes,

a blooming apple tree, lichen-embroidered.
Spilling further down the slope to Fiery Run,
a neglected orchard. Rolling hills for another

six miles westward, then the greening Shenandoahs.
The trees wavered with bees, and as far as
they could see, a lacework of blossoms, old bark,

new green leaves like little licks of fire, grass, and the
white airy seedpods of dandelion. They kissed,
moved apart, kissed, renewing and enlarging

their sensations until they were pure creatures, neither
human nor other, but beyond themselves. The lichen,
silver when they first arrived, turned turquoise, then

greyish-green. Because such a day changes one forever,
when they rose and dressed and returned to the city,
then drove back to their apartments, one northward,

another eastward—it seemed as if each, through the days
to come, carried a glass sphere near the center
of the body, a sphere filled with a liquid metal

like mercury that splashed silver whenever each took
a step. They could not say what it was they carried—
perhaps the dream of a child they might bear,

or what it was they hoped to engender in one another.
They knew it as gift, as blessing, as the long-sought
and now-befallen. They simply stepped carefully,
so as not to wake a sleeping god.

Chelsea

It happens
we are half-naked
in the back room
on a fold-out bed
in Chelsea.

—Alcohol.
He is on his side.
I am on mine.
And we are talking
in Chelsea.

The idea
would have been absurd
at home, but here
in New York City
in Chelsea

it crosses
my mind but only
for a moment
before we both move
over, on our own,
in Chelsea.

God and the G-Spot

"He didn't want to believe. He wanted to know."
– Ann Druyan, Carl Sagan's wife, on why he didn't believe in God

I want to know too. Belief and disbelief
are a pair of tourists standing on swollen feet
in the Prado—*I don't like it.*
I do.—before the Picasso.

Or the tattoo artist with a silver stud
in her full red executive lips,
who, as she inked in the indigo blue, said,
I think the G-spot's one of those myths
men use to make us feel inferior.

God, the G-spot, falling in love. The earth round
and spinning, the galaxies speeding
in the glib flow of the Hubble expansion.
I'm an East Coast Jew. We all have our opinions.

But it was in the cabin at La Selva Beach
where I gave her the thirty tiny red glass hearts
I'd taken back from my husband when I left.
He'd never believed in them. She, though, scooped
them up like water, let them drip through her fingers
like someone who has so much she can afford to waste.

That's the day she reached inside me
for something I didn't think I had.
And like pulling a fat shining trout from the river
she pulled the river out of me. That's
the way I want to know God.

Poem for a New Girlfriend

I'm driving down the highway in the dark
on my way to pick you up,
with the ocean on one side
and raindrops spattering the windshield,
balancing a coke between my legs.
If a baby were asleep in the front seat
nothing would wake it,
not the hiss of the long grass
waving by the sea wall,
not the cypress branches groaning in the wind
or the dim necklaces of surf
tumbling onto the sand.

I'm afraid to do anything sudden
on this wet pavement,
afraid to change direction or speed up,
to give you the small bracelet
I bought today in the Castro
or to say anything about the future,
as though the car might slide sideways
or the doors fly open.
So the baby would go on sleeping,
a pale shadow beside me,
stirring slightly perhaps, its hands
like stars in the glow from the dash.

Impossible to tell
what snowlit oceans
might be swaying under its eyelids,
with no cars on the road
and the lights out front
all turning green in the rain.

Sperm Count

As with sex, I did as instructed the first time. I let it
run into a sterile flask—little flood of a million or ten—

then jumped into my car & rushed it to a lab in a
hospital wing at the end of a hall. I handed it to a woman

who looked at it & frowned. *So, who are you?* she asked.
I told her, *I'm the same guy whose name is on the bottle.*

Scientists were looking through microscopes at other
men's little floods, & counting & counting.

After she took it, there was nothing else to do, my
job was done. How lonely I felt when I left her desk

& went to my car. Only minutes before I'd been on the very
point of myself. How suddenly cold were the sky & the day,

like papered-over windows of an empty store. I already
suspected the truth: I had plenty of sperm. They were

healthy, but lazy: I could populate the earth with
people who wouldn't care to get ahead. Maybe I already

knew tragedies were coming that would have nothing to do
with what vast numbers of little souls I could send forth

like Moses with his rod. I wanted to take the rest
of the day off, but knew the phone in my office had rung

while I was still at home filling that flask, men of business
wondering where I was, what the hell I was doing.

Upon Seeing an Ultrasound Photo of an Unborn Child

Tadpole, it's not time yet to nag you
about college (though I have some thoughts
on that), baseball (ditto), or abstract
principles. Enjoy your delicious,
soupy womb-warmth, do some rolls and saults
(it'll be too crowded soon), delight in your early
dreams—which no one will attempt to analyze.
For now: may your toes blossom, your fingers
lengthen, your sexual organs grow (too soon
to tell which yet) sensitive, your teeth
form their buds in their forming jawbone, your already
booming heart expand (literally
now, metaphorically later); O your spine,
eyebrows, nape, knees, fibulae,
lungs, lips.... But your soul,
dear child: I don't see it here, when
does that come in, whence? Perhaps God,
and your mother, and even I—we'll all contribute
and you'll learn yourself to coax it
from wherever: your soul which holds your bones
together and lets you live
on earth.—Fingerling, sidecar, nubbin,
I'm waiting, it's me, Dad,
I'm out here. You already know
where Mom is. I'll see you more directly
upon arrival. You'll recognize
me—I'll be the tall-seeming, delighted
blond guy, and I'll have
your nose.

Goodnight, Goodbye

I have only seen my mother in photographs
but can picture the night my father finally
charmed her into bed, or the back of his Buick—

they've returned to the parking lot: dim light reveals
a sheen of sweat on her forehead and upper-lip.
Her Scottish skin is blotchy, as if she'd had a drink.

He lights her cigarette, regards her in the match
light, but her eyes focus on the tuft of hair—
she'd kissed him there—at the open collar of his

shirt. She is trembling; it's time for her to go.
They stand by his car and he takes her hand,
kisses it; she presses her other hand to her heart.

Then they notice her blouse, something's askew—
she mismatched the top button and hole, and
they laugh. It was her first time. She thinks

he has made her a promise. He must have
known that. He leans, kisses her. Whoever,
wherever he is, he must have known that much.

Cantata, viii.

Early March, trickle and rush of ice melt in mountains;
someone says *big as a house*. In dirt, deep
bulbs *tick*. So sharp now, I hear them sing out. *Tulips*,
my lips pucker, part, then kiss to say the word.
Iron, loam, leaf-rot and fir; fern, fog—
nostrils flare; each scent floods my head.
Round powdered shoulders, frilly pink petals,
pollen of ink black pistils and stamens—soon
to emerge: buried fists or hearts: one hundred fifty-
three beats per minute, crown-to-rump ten inches now
and over two pounds. Content, I've gained fifteen—
belly skin stretched taut, ribs I know by feel: *flutter* and
kick. Linea negra runs my length. *Tick tick;*
I borrow the meters of men I knew in school, but
my mother's was first: *systole, diastole...*
Abundance of blood and breath to forge anew. In two
months' time: bloody show of fringed parrot tulips a-
glow in round bodies—glorious, nodding, blowsy
then full-blown. *Gaia, matrix, matter*: I
rub my navel, bursting with how I've grown and grow.

The Birth Room

We stare together
at the same fixed point
where there would be a curtain
if there were a window.
We try to breathe in time.

There is a method
to standing pain.
It's breaking down.

I don't suffer.
Still I'm amazed
how soon I'm overwhelmed.

In five minutes
we can call the doctor.

The lamp is dazzling
but there's no clock,
no lock, no mirror.

I keep winding a watch.
The second hand won't move.

A glass of water clouds
where you sipped it
a second, an hour ago.

When the nurse enters
with the stethoscope
it's as if we never doubted
and we hear the heartbeat—

command after command
in an unknown language,
directing us to be happy,

to be mother and father,
to grow old, to be loved,

to wait all our lives
for a single moment.

Arrival

After Christopher Smart

I will consider my son William,
who came into the world two weeks early, as if he couldn't wait;
who was carried on a river that gushed from his mother;
who was purple with matted black hair;
who announced his arrival not by crying but by peeing, with the
    umbilical cord still attached;
who looked all around with wide slate-blue eyes and smacked
    his lips as if to taste the world;
who took to his mother's breast right away;
who sucks my little finger with such vigor that it feels as if
    he's going to pull my fingernail right off;
who sometimes refuses my finger, screwing up his face in disgust
    as if I have stuck a pickled radish into his mouth;
whose face is beautiful and not like a shriveled prune;
whose hair, though black, is soft as milkweed;
who was born with long eyelashes that girls will someday envy;
whose fingernails are minuscule, thin and pliable;
whose toes are like caterpillars;
whose penis is a little acorn;
whose excrement is like the finest mustard;
who can squeak like a mouse and bleat like a lamb;
who hiccups and his whole body convulses;
who screams and turns red and kicks sometimes when we change
    his diaper;
who when he stops screaming is probably peeing;
whose deep sobs from the back of his throat bring tears
    to my own eyes;
who likes to be carried in a pouched sling;
who thinks he is a marsupial;
who has soft fur on his shoulders, back, and legs;
who is nocturnal and whose eyes are widest at night;
who will sleep sometimes if I lay him across my chest;
whose eyes flutter, whose nostrils dilate, and whose mouth
    twitches into strange grimaces and smiles as he dreams;

who is full of the living spirit which causes his body to wiggle
    and squirm;
who stretches his arms and arches his back and you can feel his
    great strength;
who lies with the soles of his feet together, as if praying with
    his feet;
who is a blessing upon our household and upon the world;
who doesn't know where the world ends and he begins;
who is himself the world;
who has a sweet smell.

New York, 1927

This time it's true, as much as I remember
from what she told me. How she gave birth
in their tenement and it took nearly two days.
In America she was Mary, always Mary,
all those hours begging her namesake
for help, the midwife muttering about
going home, thinking *this one's dead*, with
the baby wedged between her narrow hips,
a cross on the wall, her arms gripping
the sheets. Years later I understood
what she meant. How she drifted
in and out, like being on a boat in fog,
rowing, drifting, but called away from
everyone she knew toward a wilderness.
As if she had to go out alone to meet
the child and bring him through not
just with her body, but some other
part of her searching at the same time.
Of course she prayed, she knew
what it smelled like to be that close
to death and she wanted to live,
and to get the baby out alive, her firstborn
who unlocked her for the others.
In the next room her husband and his
father heard the child cry and could
finally feel their own sickness and fear
overtaking them, maybe they'd been drinking,
maybe it was her father-in-law's red hair,
but she remembered him coming into
the bedroom just as a familiar darkness
began refilling her belly. How spent
she felt while his eyes looked wild
with confusion for his first grandson
and what it had cost her, and though she knew
she was alive, he looked strange to her
as a being from the other world and put

his hands into his pockets and pulled
the cloth out so all his money fell—no
she said he threw it—onto her bed,
silver coins landing around her legs,
the white insides of his pockets flapped
out like tiny wings at his hips. He called in
all his sons—my stunned grandfather
and his unmarried brothers—and pointed
to my father sleeping on the bed all
washed and wrapped in white by
the midwife. *Now*, he told the men,
you work only for him.

Latching On, Falling Off

I. When She Takes My Body into Her Body

She comes to me squirming in her father's arms,
gumming her fingers, her blanket, or rooting
on his neck, thrashing her mouth from side to side
to raise a nipple among his beard hairs. My shirt sprouts
two dark eyes; for three weeks she's been outside me,
and I cry milk to hear my baby—any baby—cry.

In the night, she smells me. From her bassinette
she wakes with a squall, her mouth impossibly huge,
her tongue aquiver with anger the baby book says
she doesn't have, aquiver like the clapper of a bell.
Her passion I wasn't prepared for, her need
naked as a sturgeon with a rippling, red gill.

Who named this letdown, this tingling upswing?
A valve twists, the thin opalescence spurts past the gate,
then comes the hindcream to make my baby creamyfat.
I fumble with one hand at my bra, offer the target
of my darkened nipple, with the other hand steady
her too-heavy head. She clamps on, the wailing ceases.

No one ever mentioned she's out for blood. I wince
as she tugs milk from ducts all the way to my armpits.
It hurts like when an angry sister plaits your hair.
It hurts like that, and like that you desire it.
Soon, soon—I am listening—she swallows,
and a layer of pain kicks free like a blanket.

Tethered, my womb spasms, then, lower, something shivers.
Pleasure piggybacks the pain, though it, too,
isn't mentioned, not to the child, drunk and splayed
like a hobo, not to the sleeping husband, innocent beside us.
Let me get it right so I remember: Once, I bared my chest
and found an animal. Once, I was delicious.

II. First Night Away from Claire

I forget to pack my breast pump,
a novelty not in any shop
here at the beach, just snorkel tubes,
shark teeth, coconut-shell bikini tops.
Should we drive back? I'm near-drunk
from my first beer in months. We've got
a babysitter, a hotel room, and on the horizon
a meteor shower promised. We've planned
slow sex, sky watch, long sleep.
His hand feels good low on my back,
tracing my lizard tattoo. And he can help—
he's had quick sips before—so we stay,
rubbing tongues, butter-dripping shrimp.

Later, he tries gamely, but it's not sexy,
not at all—he needs to suck a glassful
from each breast. The baby's so much better.
He rests. It's hot, he says, and sweet.
We're tired. We fall asleep.
I wake pre-dawn from pain.

Those meteors we forgot to watch—
it will be thirty years
before they pass this way again.

III. After Weaning, My Breasts Resume Their Lives
as Glamour Girls

Initially hesitant, yes,
but once called into duty,
they never looked back.

Models-turned-spokeswomen,
they never dreamed they'd have so much to say.
They swelled with purpose,

mastered that underwater tongue,

translating the baby's long-vowel cries
and oozing their answer,

tidal, undeniable, fulfilled.
For a year, they let the child draw forth
that starry river, as my friend Ann has termed it—

then, it was time, stopped the flow.
They are dry now, smaller, tidy, my nipples
the lighter, more fetching pink.

The bras ugly as Ace bandages,
thick-strapped, trap-doored,
too busy for beauty—

and the cotton pads lining them
until damp, then yeasting in the hamper—
all have been washed and stored away.

So I'm thinking of how,
when World War II had ended,
the factory-working wives

were fired, sent home
to care for returning soldiers,
when my husband enters the bedroom—

Aren't you glad? he asks, glad,
watching me unwrap bras
tissue-thin and decorative

from the tissue of my old life,
watching, worshipfully, the breasts resettle
as I fasten his red favorite—

Aren't you glad? He's walking
toward them, addressing them, it seems—
but, Darling, they can't answer,

poured back into their old mold,

muffled beneath these lovely laces,
relearning how it feels, seen and not heard.

IV. It Was a Strange Country

where I lived with my daughter while I fed her
from my body. It was a small country, an island for two,
and there were things we couldn't bring with us,
like her father. He watched from the far shore,
well-meaning, useless. Sometimes I asked
for a glass of water, so he had something to give.

The weather there was overcast, volatile.
We were tied to the tides of whimper and milk,
the flotsam of spit-up, warm and clotted,
on my neck, my thigh. Strange: I rarely minded,
I liked the yogurt smell trapped beneath her chinfolds.
How soon her breath bloomed sweet again.

She napped, my ducts refilled
like veins of gold that throb though lodged in rock.
When she woke, we adjusted our body language.
How many hours did she kiss one breast or the other?
I told her things. She tugged my bottom lip,
like sounds were coins beneath my fascinating tongue.

We didn't get many tourists, much news—
behind the closed curtains, rocking in the chair,
the world was a rumor all summer. All autumn.
All winter, in which she sickened, sucked for comfort,
a cord of snot between her nose, my breast.
Her small pillows of breath. We slept there, single-bodied.

Then came spring and her milk teeth and her bones
longer in my lap, her feet dangling, and, rapt,
she watched me eat, scholar of sandwiches and water.
Well, I knew the signs. I held her tight, I waded out,
I swam us away from that country, swam us back
to my husband pacing the shore, yelling and waving,

in his man fists, baby spoons that flashed, cupping suns.
It was a strange country that we returned to, separately—
strange, but not for long. Soon, the milk stops
simmering and the child forgets the mother's taste,
so the motherland recedes on the horizon,
a kindness—we return to it only at death.

First Nightmare Waking

What is the world at night-time,
and where does the daytime world go?
She kicks back her blanket and whimpers,
the monitor crackling me awake.

The window's cube of black light glimmers
back its own dark language at two a.m.
In the indistinguishable outside, a refrain
of summer frogs undulates from the woods.

One night, she cries only for her mother.
One night, she cries only for her father.
What can I do but lumber up and stagger
to her side, to hold her tiny hands?

This is the world at two and a half years old:
as I shamble to her new bedside, for Anastasia
to whimper in all the language she knows,
"Papa, the witch is bothering me."

I watch an infant grow into a child,
the child grow slowly from fearlessness
into fear, as if the boundary of fear
is a country one learns to cross into.

Over months, a slow hesitancy
blooms behind her umber eyes.
In our warm parlor of birth and sharing,
I move as usual to rewind the movie.

But Anastasia guides my hand away
from her favorite videos, and whispers,
*"I can't watch no more, Papa.
It a little bit too scary now."*

And oddly, it's my voice which protests,
"But you love the scarecrow, the tin-man,
the witch is your favorite funny voice..."
But nothing stays the same. Everything

moves in the dark now. Her bedroom becomes
a cave, her open closet a mouth for devouring,
the walls accomplices for creaking—
and all the dark that moves in the corner.

I want to cradle her and tell her—
Look, the evening is only the lush
violet of my own father, the loved flower.
The deep evening is an orchard of sleep.

In that moment of murky rocking,
I gaze upon her curly head, see how
much she's growing, despite my holding her.
All I can do is sway and hum, and ask myself,

What is this world at night-time,
and where does the regular world go?
I don't want her to age or grow
out of letting me cuddle her.

Instead, all I can reasonably do
is to simply be there rocking her
back to sleep at 3 a.m, whispering,
Come to the wide bed of comfort, child.

Nestle curled in Papa's arms
for night to pass you securely through.
In a world yet safe, dark is but sleeping.
In a father's arms, there are no witches.

Cathedral

For hours I held one of my son's infant twins
as she slept. For a little time, before we knew
who each would be, it didn't matter which
soft sweaty newborn head lay on my breast
ruining my velvet shirt. There was nothing else
in all the world I wanted. As on approach
to Chartres: it's been there centuries, you merely
have not known it. Now you know
nothing can prepare you for the way it rises
from the hills. It stands, imperfect, beautiful.
Nothing is required of you, and everything.

First Empathy

The pig on the page is crying.
Its back is angled toward the reader,
but we can still see the squinch
of its features in profile, the three
huge tears gushing diagonally upward.
Its kite is stuck in the tree.
And from somewhere below the crown
of her head, an inch from my lips,
my daughter cries out: "Yeah! Yeah! *Yeah!*"
She is pointing frantically at the pig,
at the kite, using the only one
of her fifteen words that comes close:
"Yeah! Yeah! *Yeah!*" as if to say
I've been there! I know this!
Story of my LIFE!
Her eighteen months' worth of sorrow
wells up in her throat, stuck there
like that kite with its diamond shape
that turns out not to be one,
even diamonds are not shaped like diamonds,
and hearts, it's all going to accrete so slowly,
the midden of quotidian disappointment,
wadding up the string and crumpling
the kite and blocking the passage
of her future joys, for life, hers and
mine to be spent watching. Now
the finger-in-the-dike wail:
she's actually holding back sobs
for this dumb little pig wearing shorts
and I can't stop this. Can't retrieve the kite.
I try to turn the page, but she slaps it back down
with a peremptory dumpling hand.
"Yeah! Yeah! *Yeah!*" One sob.
But there are other pictures of pigs,
I say idiotically, happy pink pigs
eating roast beef and smiling ones

who run their own deli counters
selling low-salt turkey instead of ham,
and pigs with snazzy convertibles,
pigs with jobs on ladders painting,
important pigs running for the bus
bearing briefcases, vacationing pigs
in green jeeps, look! Nothing doing.
She has identified this page as hers.
"Yeah! Yeah!" That kite is stuck in the tree.
"Yeah!" We both sit here and stare.
Christ. It is never going to come down.

August Horizon

The canoe picks up speed
and forges north with the weight
of our bodies and the thwarts
and the folded tent
and the ash paddles, the prow
cuts its notch in the sky
and my daughter points to the riverbank
and says "house," "tree," "bird,"
though she never used the words before
she pronounces them calmly
as if they were always there,
on shore: here at Little Falls
the stars bend with the jay stroke,
the dipper becomes a funnel, the plough
a jackknife, and when the moon rises
in a new part of the forest
abolishing all degrees of shadow
the child says "night."

Query

Who left
this wooly caterpillar
on the counter, sliced
lengthwise? Who left this
symmetrical filet to dry
beside my best steak knife?
My son says he wondered
"what's inside, what makes it go?"
And left it there
because now he knows.

At the Crematorium, My Son Asks
Why We're All Wearing Black

These days the system is state of the art—scrims of smoke,
no odor. At least the neighbors don't protest
and the birds still gather on the tarred roof's edge
to feed on seeds pooled at drain tiles. We accumulate
and are dispersed at the traffic light out front, while within
this relay point of caskets and morgue lockers,
the husks of our fallen continue their diminishment.

We're all members of this committee, son. We serve
with our tanks full and our tops down
until in one moment
we are reduced to manila envelopes
of movie stubs, bus transfers and address books;
in another, to pollen ruffling
the overcast, distended cloud cover of the world.

The passing lanes, the turn signals, the green and yellow lights,
the no U-turn and school crossing signs,
they all lead here.

You're old enough, now, for one dark suit and tie,
and to know exactly why
you're uncomfortable wearing it.

My Son's Wedding, My Daughter's

Within five weeks
I heard both children say
what only the young can say
about what they'll love
for the rest of their lives.

Almost all of us
who've spoken like that
have needed, years later, to edit, retract,
change the object or verb,
insert a *mostly* or *except when*,
compensating for a life lived
too intensely or not enough.

Thus the churches were full
of stepsiblings, middle-aged singles,
and my children's friends in various states
of married or miserable,
too young to know the difference.

Present also, their father,
to whom, thirty years earlier,
I'd promised my life and, beside him,
his wife and her children.
Behind them my best friend
on her third marriage,
a cousin twice divorced,
a niece with a broken heart.

I stood at one ceremony, then the other,
aware that a wedding
might be the worst time
to think about the future,
its inevitable revisions.
Next to me the man
I'd married just months before

kept his arm around my waist.
What could any of us do
except raise a glass,
no, not as a toast to hope,
but to the uncomplicated joy
with which my children spoke:
I do, I will, I promise.

First Night in the New House

As if this were our honeymoon again, the man I've slept with
eighteen years carried me over the doorstep
(but not up the seventeen stairs), and in our new bed

we lay awake till two, amazed
at the height of our ceilings and the way
the fan over the bed so silently mused.

Giddy at the light
tint of blue we'd painted the walls and the mirrored
closet doors that expanded the room, we knew

how silly we were to believe that the act
of sleeping and waking in this new room
would make a difference in our lives—

as on the first day of school each year
we would take out our sharpened number two's
and open our unused loose-leafs

as if to enter the first page of our lives.
Even then we understood how it must have felt
biting into the controversial, overrated apple.

First Date in Twenty-Five Years

Buttoning my sweater over the huge splotch
of white wine splashed on to neutralize the coin

of red dribbled earlier in my nerves, I sit down
across the table from this man for the first time

and find I've forgotten how to use a fork.
Returning home, I set the story we might make

beside the story I am making, then alternate the two
like fitful sleep positions. To the first I give lots of room

and no punctuation; from the second I subtract
destruct, add *self.* Doze off feeling kissed. Morning

proper finds me weeping into bathwater: I must turn
into the one I've been threatening to become, faster.

Poem on My Birthday

In the first snowflake imprinting the kitchen window by the sink
my mother, eighty-three, can see the features of the night
I left her for the world. But in this star—
since that is how the prism arranges itself, shimmering—
we are still one body. In an hour from this glimpse
my knocking for release will expel me to the future.
What are we now? She stretches her fingers to her belly,
containing the first kick I will issue from. She remembers:
this is all we are—another night before the window,
summer now and the cicadas beyond the screen
invisible and rasping, drive fissures in the dark
to open for her soul, longing to fly out.
She will not go. She is two souls here
and for awhile she must put off all the world
while I am still inside her. And afterward
wonder the discontent she fed a child
as her own, this man-child never satisfied
while satisfaction, a demon she deliberately puts on,
divides them as she never wished. And so she weeps.
I imagine her tonight especially as she weeps.

FOUR

Evidence of Life

(Summer, 1971)

Correct temperatures, perfect sweetness,
crusts, crumbs, juices.
The universe is baking, round with fire,
planetary pavilions of white hats
with the secrets of making apple crisp,
military recipe of the day in my green box
like grass or everything we own.
Every U.S. Army enlisted man
has apple crisp today, my first time
with the thing. From Hanoi to Helsinki,
or wherever men are military, this
chance to smack on sugar will be
a break between bullets, boredom,
snakes, flies, cake dry shit, jeeps,
helicopters, M-16's, M-59 grenades
or the standard issue combat knives
that can disembowel, slice the pie crust
evenly or not so evenly, the jagged
edge making a mess of softness.

Every green box has instructions,
a little this, a little that, a little
Make it up if you don't know how
as well as the secrets visible only to
mess people praying for success,
silent in prayer before apple crisp.

On the table it looks back at me,
sighing a little to let out the air of being
held under fire and then lets itself open,
the juices escaping over the hot skin,
thinking to itself... *from seed to this.*

Each Sound

Beginnings are brutal, like this accident
of stars colliding, mute explosions
of colorful gases, the mist and dust
that would become our bodies
hurling through black holes, rising,
muck-ridden, from pits of tar and clay.
Back then it was easy to have teeth,
claw our way into the trees—it was
accepted, the monkeys loved us, sat
on their red asses clapping and laughing.
We've forgotten the luxury of dumbness,
how once we crouched naked on an outcrop
of rock, the moon huge and untouched
above us, speechless. Now we talk
about everything, incessantly,
our moans and grunts turned on a spit
into warm vowels and elegant consonants.
We say *plethora*, *demitasse*, *ozone* and *love*.
We think we know what each sound means.
There are times when something so joyous
or so horrible happens our only response
is an intake of breath, and then
we're back at the truth of it,
that ball of life expanding
and exploding on impact, our heads,
our chests, filled with that first
unspeakable light.

The Middle Age

Between TV and computer screens
counterfeiting a dragon glow in our mouths agog
and fundamentalists dreaming up real
fire and smoke to transmogrify the U.S.A.,

we may be on our way to something else,
as people in the Middle Ages sensed the decay
of the feudal system. Little orange mushrooms
sprouted from castle mortar and lilies

festered, till BOOM, the Gutenberg Bible
blew the roof off the church. The big party
(individualism) began, and the bare naked
rodeo we now call the Renaissance

gave us—let's face it—the best art ever.
In 1620 F. Bacon posited three
inventions as the high tech hocus-pocus
behind society's sea change: printing, gunpowder,

and the magnet. That's right, the magnet.
Used in compasses, it made heavenly bodies
obsolete, thus exploration of the New
World easy as pie. I mention in passing

Columbus's packs of mastiffs and greyhounds
trained on human flesh (brown), but the main
needle that guides my life is the needle
of debt. True North: My Mortgage. I find myself

thinking of Las Vegas, where I might
bathe in lilac neon and wander
palaces, tickled by the bickering
roulette wheels and the final clicks.

And get free drinks. And catch a lion act.
And I would turn my back on all that,
sagely, and walk out in the desert,
letting my crow's feet crinkle ironically.

Out in the desert at sunset
the wind must sequin up a sand grain
or two, and the prodigal pruneface moon
appear above a dune. Beautiful.

Poignant as hell. And I bet you can hear,
far-off, barking Lotto numbers
the Beast of the Apocalypse. Yes, yes,
a Vegas vacation might be just the thing. Yes,

but I recall my childhood most keenly:
Hansel and Gretel's predicament: luminous
breadcrumbs one by one blinking out, a bird
too dark to be seen.

The Kildan Women

The Kildan women had never seen trees
    St. Kildan
    of Scotland's Outer Hebrides, being
        all stark cliffs, with bushes for birds' nests:
Matrons and girls dressed in goose-skins,
    feathers kept decorous by bird-bone pins,
        feet in duck bills glued to blocks of rock.
Their record for chastity reached back
    five thousand years unblemished,

Until a reckless picnic on the woodsy
    Isle of Skye
    filled them per local story
        with mischievous inspiration, those sleek
piously upthrust trunks, those green
    frenzies of kiss, guess and intense
        fragility, the leaves, which taught them
ways to blend interest with modesty, shed
    bird-bone pins and stone-hoofed boots,

Wear dresses tight as the trees' rough shells
    called bark
    for the men and dogs' raw coughing,
        while haddock in St. Kildan's Bay
lifted their silver heads, singing *'Hey! Hey! Hey!'*
    for now all could nibble each other instead of—
        dead worms on murderous hooks
tied to strings of doom and the bread-crumbs of destiny.
    The rest is the chaos of history.

Self-Portrait as a Drowned Man

So hard to keep the body still, early photography studios
were torture chambers, filled with devices to hold the body

long enough for the film to be exposed, and so when
Hippolyte Bayard took off his shirt, aimed the camera,

and posed himself, eyes closed and body leaning slightly
against a chair to make it heavy, to give it the stillness

of a corpse, it's probable he fell asleep, so unblurred is
his torso with clasped hands, his combed wet hair.

Bayard claims on the back of the 1840 photograph
that the body is drowned, tells how

the French government overlooked him for Daguerre
and how no one claimed the body from the morgue,

photography's first self-portrait a faked suicide with a note ending:
"Ladies and Gentlemen, pass on lest he offend your sense of smell."

When I first saw death I felt my body freeze, I felt how hard
to keep the mind still, how hard to understand, relive,

undo the moment when the falling body
made no sound, a split-second in the corner of my eye,

then nothing in the chalky sky but the tip of an apartment building.
Then a gasping, then the body hidden by a circle of bystanders

taking uneven steps back as the blood began to pool,
as the blood itself grew fingers

releasing something that cold February morning.
So hard to hold the body still, at the stairway to the metro

my breath billowed out. A policeman grabbed my shoulders
and yelled for me to stop, he held me there

to keep me and the rest of the crowd away from the body,
yelled *"Arrêtez!"* while the blood on the pavement

became a kind of cursive, a story told
on the sidewalk's pages of dying and exposure.

To the South

*(Composer Fanny Mendelssohn-Hensel, sister
of Felix Mendelssohn, travels to Italy for the first time)*

The journey to Italy began in your youth
   among vaulted cliffs of the Saint Gotthard Pass,
its rock-scrabbled trail through thundering Reuss gorge
   of the Swiss alps softening to flowering
meadow-valleys and the green hills of Andermatt,
   glaciered mountains just beyond so proximate
     to Italian soil it recast the natives' speech.

In a letter to your cousin you imagined,
   if a young man, you'd have walked alone
those final miles to the border, freed from constraint
   or concern for who'd accompany you,
to where *the plain adorns itself*—corn grass, aloe,
   olive tree and cypress, one fair, one dark—poised
     in blue air, and sun poured like wine across the fields.

You'd wait seventeen years, Felix's letters
   quickening with the promise: to arrive in Rome,
city of ruins, art remaking each fissure,
   city of sacred music, masses and plainchant
echoing towards you as you strained to draw near
   the wrought iron grill of the Sistine Chapel,
     its ceiling, walls, flushed with color and sound.

When Carnival arrived you surprised yourself,
   took to the streets with munitions of sweetmeats,
flowers to throw at the revelers that climbed
   the running board of your coach, elegant masks
muting their lighthearted words, costumes like paint
   spattering the path of the Corso, fantasies
     and farces play-acted to bedlam and noise—

so unlike the Villa Medici's serene façade,
   its precise ornamentation home
to the Académie de France, where Gounod
   and Bousquet listened raptly to your Bach,
sought your knowledge of German composition,
   your talents so admired in those hushed rooms
      that you, in excitement, couldn't stop composing.

An incomparable musician and pianist
   Gounod later wrote, *her intelligence revealed
in deep eyes and a fiery gaze*, his words
   marking open your path like a milestone,
your confidence unsheathed like those insouciant
   blooms softening the stiff geometry
      of the Medici gardens' array of hedge

and statuary, groves where you rehearsed
   musicians in the rich afternoon sun
for intimate evening concerts—lights in town,
   fireflies, a church illuminating soft air—
or wrote, the melodies, harmonic progressions,
   forming to words with precision and ease,
      of the south... land of eternal blossom.

La Bajada

Driving north before Cochiti exit, he visualizes
a bleeding anthropologist pulled from a wrecked car

but encounters only starlight and wind. Tonight
cars glide past him at eighty. Marine biologists

believed the coelacanth was extinct until a fisherman
off Madagascar pulled one up in a net. After 40,000

photographs in a bubble chamber, technicians had no track
of omega minus and wanted to quit. Sometimes luck

and sometimes perseverance. In the morning he woke
to agapanthus odor, felt presence and absence

resemble an asymptotic line and curve that squeeze
closer and closer but do not touch. He glances up

at Casseopeia arcing toward the north-northwest,
wonders if mosquito eggs in the pond are about to hatch,

sees her trim red and orange ranunculi on the counter.
And as he pushes on the gas and begins to ascend

La Bajada, water runs in the acequia
behind the kitchen porch for the first time this year.

First Sight

A blind woman—who by some miracle can
no longer hear the dirty snow bank shrinking
and melting like soapsuds because her eyes

are full-up—stands fixed and faint at her window:
the barn drawn so close, the cat—how could
he be so bright, how could he have pinned

between his paws at this moment some poor
creature—what would death look like instead
of smell? But no, it's stiff and rough, this thing

her eyes have no name for, which he joyously
tosses about, as if to celebrate her moment of first
sight—it's bark, a bit of tree!—and pieces

of tree from all sides assemble and crowd
into her new vision, or is it the eyes that do this,
gathering together long-fingered bare hands grasping

for sky—which she thinks must be cloud-white not
blue, judging by dirty snow and clean cat, not exactly
a color but aching with brightness. The clouds say

nothing of what's behind them, the way they glare
down on the amazing semi-transparency of ice—
and she wonders what diamonds do, fingers

her pearls, and there are her hands—not white at all,
budding from red sleeves: would blood look like that
or fire? Her eyes molten in their orbits, hungry

for house-bound things, memorized by touch,
so whole now they hurt like a new pleasure:
the saxophone aglow on the rug, the party

the afghan makes on the bed, her own features
aslant in a watery mirror: recognition ringing
in her fingers—terrain of mother! Oh, salty

waterfall, loud window: that never-seen
curve of lip, those smooth teeth, this
yes red spurt of bird in sudden sun—

Bridge View

The grandeur of the tower was nothing at first
but our surmise at what it would become,
gleaned from rumors; though before long
we watched the stanchions' gradual ascent
above Shore Road's distant stand of trees
where Third narrowed to its vanishing point.

Nothing at first, and then, from the corner,
one day we saw the legs barely risen,
two sheer columns of iron and steel:
the tensile thighs of a man being built
foot by lifted foot from the bottom up,
girder and crossbeam, rivet and plate.

For two years he grew, his height accruing
like a child's stature notched on a wall,
while up from the Narrows the body took form
from foot to hips and vaulted crotch. But where
was the rest of him, broad torso and head?
It was we who gave that image to the air,

gave it likewise to its twin across the strait
before they strung the cables, hung the roadway
amazingly into place, so that, that first time,
we drove through a space left by torn-down homes
up the approach, the Island spread before us,
the river below, and we climbed into the sky.

First Job Viper

Whose clay courts did he water and roll?

Whose golf greens did he lather and shave?

Whose command to kill a snake did he obey?

Whose fear of the local did he despise?

Whose price on his life did he suddenly realize?

Whose blood to this day does he plot to poison?

First Turtle

(Wolf Lake State Fish Hatchery)

I'd never killed one before. I guess the best way
is to shoot them in the head with a twenty-two. But since one fears
what one does not necessarily know
how to do, I was in a hurry to get the slaughtering
over with. I sharpened a hatchet until it gleamed
then waited for the turtle to stick his head out again. The
hit was clean but I missed
the neck and the hatchet sunk into the turtle's skull.

When I was done I was blood splattered. The head lay dead
in the dirt but the body continued to move, not like a chicken
going crazy, but like a turtle with no head
simply trying to walk away. I picked him up by the tail
and stuck him upside down in a bucket to drain. When I
      returned much later
I found the bucket on its side and the turtle was gone.
He was fifty yards away on one of the dikes walking in circles.

Taking Calls in Freeport, NY

Sometimes I thought I might
gasp my last breath at N.Y. Tel.,
but went on intoning
the lion is busy, please call again.
Plugged into a board,
headset snapped over my ears,
to drunks' cracked voices on the line,
to anyone possessed of a dime,
I asked: "your number, please,"
again and again.
A supervisor had told me:
"rhyme nine with lion,
five with die of."
The first year I lived
on my own, learned to please men
without getting undressed,
checked out books
from the library: *Anna Karenina*
and *House of the Dead*, I swallowed
two bottles of Anacin but groggily woke
in my rooming house to turn eighteen.
The next night on the job,
I ripped the cords
out by their stems, left them
in a tangled heap, imagined lips
shouting: "operator, operator,
I've been cut off,"
across the local wires
and into my last hour of taking calls
in the island towns.

Second Story Warehouse
(Summer, 1966)

Come with me to the second story warehouse
   where I filled orders for the factory downstairs,
and commanded the freight elevator, and read
   high in the air on a floating carpet of boxes.

I could touch the damp pipes in the ceiling
   and smell the rust. I could look over
the Puerto Rican workers in the parking lot,
   smoking and laughing and kidding around

in Spanish during their break, especially Julia,
   who bit my lower lip until it bruised and bled,
and taught me to roll cigarettes in another language,
   and called me her virgin boy from the suburbs.

All summer I read Neruda's *Canto General*
   and took lessons from Juan, who trained me
to accept orders with dignity—*dignidad*—
   and never take any shit from the foreman.

He showed off the iron plate in his skull
   from a bar fight with a drunken supervisor,
while the phone blinked endlessly from Shipping
   & Handling, and light glinted off the forklift.

I felt like a piece of wavy, fluted paper
   trapped between two sheets of linerboard
in the Single Wall, double-faced boxes
   we lifted and cursed, sweated and stacked

on top of heavy wooden skids. I dreaded
   the large, unwieldy, industrial A-flutes
and the 565 stock cartons that we carried
   in bundles through the dusty aisles

while downstairs a line of blue collars fed
    slotting, gluing, and stitching machines.
Juan taught me about mailers and multidepths,
    and praised the torrential rains of childhood,

the oysters that hid in the bloody coral,
    their pearls shimmering in the twisted rock,
green stones polished by furious storms
    and coconut palms waving in the twilight.

He praised the sun that floats over the island
    like a bell ringed with fire, or a sea rose,
and the secret torch that forever burns
    inside us, a beacon that no one can touch.

Come with me to the second story warehouse
    where I learned how to squat and lift,
how to reach Die-cuts and Five-panel folders,
    and saw the iron shine inside a skull.

Every day at precisely three in the afternoon
    we delivered our orders to the loading dock.
We may go down dusty and tired, Juan said,
    but we come back smelling like the sea.

Job

My mother sold life insurance
for twenty-five years—
something you can't see or touch.

The first day I went to work
in midtown Manhattan—
Fifth Avenue in pumps and a business suit—
I smelled the pretzel vendors
and thought of my father, elevators
carrying him up to the sixty-third floor
for fifteen years; how, one day,
they took him down with a box
of paperweights and picture frames.
Every childhood morning I'd wake
to the whir of his electric tie rack
circling outside my bedroom door.

For years that was all I wanted—a machine
I would never have a use for. I work
at the phone company this month:
ID badge, elevator bank, twelfth floor.
We document old systems
for tangible assets: file cabinets,
buildings, telephone poles, things
you can touch. My system,
SCATS, depreciates and
retires assets. Bob, my client
with the overwhelming mustache,
calls me "Brooklyn," smiles, doesn't know
we downsize, redistribute, fire people.
He has a sign on his desk:
"It's nice to be important,
but it's more important
to be nice." He waves
over the cubicle walls,

shouts, *Hey Brooklyn, you stayin'*
out of trouble?

My mother sold life insurance
for twenty-five years—not a morbid plan
for the death of a loved one,
she insisted, but fiscal reality.

The vertigo of morning
subway commuting, rushing
gears, twin headlights
blooming from the anxious tunnel, beautiful
fifteen-year-olds from the East Side projects,
lacquered hair, sneakers, enormous
hoop earrings, talking in rhythmic downtown
Latina English—their effortless strength
and music rolling
like the train; fuck this
and fuck that, fuck this
and fuck that, fuck this
and fuck that, throttled forward.

The security guard with the blank freckled face
forgets me when I forget my pass, claims
she's never seen me before.
I believe her. Express elevator,
slate blue cubicle near aisle B,
pumps, blouse, slacks,
clips, staples, tacks. Fist of fire
in my stomach. This job makes me want
to frequent upscale restaurants, devour
thermostats, bleed like a tattoo,
barter for angels. As if I have nothing
to lose.

My mother sold life insurance
for twenty-five years—she was certified
by the state and always told me,
If you can sell that, you can sell anything.

Working past ten, I'm allowed to return
in a company taxi, sliding around
on the leather of the black backseat,
East River speeding by with the rhythm
of FDR Drive: fuck this and fuck that,
endless buildings winking wealth,
shrinking slowly as we drive the Brooklyn Bridge
to my walk-up studio on the other side
where I'll climb six flights to eat
filet mignon rescued from a client dinner,
distributed to the Analysts by a kindly Partner,
on my Salvation Army couch in pajamas,
watching the 11 o'clock news blaring
the unstoppable market.

First Time Reading Freud

My copy of his *Introductory Lectures*
had an odor I couldn't place, an organic,
vaguely fleshy... pulpy... baby wipes-
type smell—though not exactly. At 18
I was having trouble concentrating,
though the words, according to theory
were processing themselves in my unconscious
while I kept track of girls in miniskirts
wafting in and out of Olin Library
like wide-winged tropical birds. I'd glance down
at Freud's bleak head floating on the cover,
half in stark shadow, monocle in place,
then gaze across the room at a Korean beauty
whose virtually flat face had gotten her
some modeling jobs, and covers of her own.
She promised her mother she'd wear pantyhose
every day, to help keep out the boys—
as if we'd get inside by accident.
I put my nose to Freud, bent the spine back
deeper to smell...an infant's soft moist head?
...a mother's breast dusted with talc?

I learned about the promise to her mother
when I pointed to new packages of hose
stacked tall on a chair by her bed.
I don't know how I got into her room
or how Freud's language crept into my head—
super ego, pleasure principle,
displacement, latent and *manifest*
and all that ugly Oedipus business—
babies with sex and murder on the brain,
little Viennese girls hard-wired
to admire their first glimpse of *zomething egstra,*
yet why hadn't I touched mine till I was 16,
and why did our professor have to tell us
about the woman he saw at Woodstock

lifting her naked baby to manipulate
his penis in her mouth, both mother
and son cooing, he said, with pleasure?
Does anybody see a problem here?
he asked an amphitheater full of freshmen.
Manipulate was the verb he used. Spackling
putty—that's what that book smelled like.

The First Time I Robbed Tiffany's

The first time I robbed Tiffany's it was raining. And it was dark, and the wind was blowing. It was like the first time I had sex. The same kind of weather, the same kind of feeling. Me and the girl in the car. Just like me and the cop in the car, after he arrested me outside the store in the rain. I promised myself I would do better next time. Just like I promised the girl. Just like I promised the cop. It felt like it always felt, me and the cop, me and the girl, me and the rain, and the wind and the darkness, and the robbery I never committed, the sex I never had, the girl I never knew, the feel I never copped, and the rain the rain the rain was all I knew and all I will ever know.

First Nights

The best of all was listening to a hush
under the chandelier that never fell
and a fat box adorned with gilded masks.

As a thick curtain parted over velvet,
my father gasped. He'd left the stage for a desk
when I was born. And now first nights were holy.

A house called the Majestic and a program,
more than *shul* and prayerbook, summoned praise.
One night, an actor, fake wrinkles, white hair,

roared, but in a whisper, *all-shaking thunder.*
I shuddered. My father had scared me once,
shutting a book and crying to some storm,

Arms, arms, sword, fire. Leaning forward
that night, I clutched a linen square
but no tears came from that king until swords

I suddenly thought real, clashed for his throne.
Applause. I glanced up, seized by exit lines.
My father said, "It helps us bear God's silences,"

and I knew watching was a kind of prayer,
a make-believe you play by looking hard,
as it sustained him when, evenings at home,

dead still in thoughts about his sister lost,
he heard of cities bombed, while there, onstage,
Lear shouted, in a whisper, *mad, sweet heaven.*

First Exercise

I was swimming
because I wanted to get skinny,
having passed the age of thirty
when the body begins its gradual revenge
for all those days of inattention
it secretly begrudged all along.
So I was finally paying it my full attention,
pulling it back and forth
across the pool's width at the baby end;
standing after each lap to wait for breath
and study the excellent rhythms of the swimmers
in the roped lanes of the Olympic pool adjoining,
as the light through high, leaded windows
broke into diamonds off their wakes;
nodding in turn to my companions at this end:
two impossibly vigorous, white-capped old men
and a dark woman in a black spandex suit
that fit her like skin. I've always hated swimming
for impeccable reasons, especially since
I'm nearly blind without my contact lenses
and I didn't understand the new goggles
I bought for my new regimen did not mean
I could keep my lenses in and see new things;
so from one of my fancy underwater racing turns
I came up without them,
and touched my eyes, and looked, and felt
a rush of panic into my chest,
the shock when someone says
there's been a terrible accident
and you don't know who or what.
Of course, after a second, I thought
"It's only your contact lenses,"
but I dived for them anyway again and again,
trying to hold myself under to pet the tile
with my palms, and later, as I walked home,
the world a blur of dull color run together,

I thought of my friend diving at dusk
in that mountain lake for his daughter
and what came to him when his hands
sank into the cold mud at the bottom.

Good Morning Coffee Makes Vivid of the Vague; Suddenly You Have Hands and Eyes and Legs!

I have serious doubts the people around me
here at the coffee shop are from here.
I mean, they are imitating people. I don't
know where they come from, I've never
seen them before, but, in all fairness,
they don't seem to be trying to take over.
They are a little pushy, though, around
the Half and Half. Really, no human
would be content to look so bad. Surely
they've heard of a comb. Those clothes,
who on earth would wear them?
The tall guy with the singing shoes,
he should only wear a hat like that
if he is stone bald. As for hair,
the one sitting beside him and swaying,
her hair looks like it snagged in a fan
and had to be cut out. Still, who says
where you have to be from to appreciate
good coffee? What are they doing
when they tap those long walking
sticks together and sway in unison?
It makes me uneasy, I can't help it.
I keep my head down to attract
little if any attention. Over the years,
I have become skilled in this way.
If you looked in here at me now,
you wouldn't know that I've come upon
something worthy of national query.
Then again, I'm no stoolie, no party-
pooper, I got my pride: "I'll see you
guys tomorrow." Maybe tomorrow
I'll get the nerve up to ask the guy
where he got the singing shoes.

Of Marilyn, and Marijuana

What is this familiar power, I wondered
    when marijuana first expanded
        the core of my torso and an inner
        Laocoon arose to stretch steel-
    belted automobile tires
        from within. Likewise the voice
        of Peter Pan's guardian fairy

(Myself) tinkled for me as I galloped like a
    dinosaur, my external spinal platters
        clattering, after Marilyn Monroe
        across a yellow pasture,
    colliding off-target high
        on her vanilla custard thigh,
        whispering to myself, haven't you

Tried this somewhere, sometime before?
    I go back to the site of banana slices
        bobbing amid Cheerios in sweet milk,
        my mother called to work one Saturday
    early, entrusting me
        to a downstairs' neighbor lady
        slumbering, how well I remember,

In the dusky buff, so that my tender naked
    four-year-old foot hoofed into her
        fur like a pony grazing,
        big toe its cold nose nuzzling
    under sage brush
        for a nourishing touch or crunch.
        How well I remember that sense

And scent of dew my little foot tickled down there,
    as she sprang like a wildcat
        and hissed like a rattler,
        "Don't do that!" how my mother

henceforward
        checked my hands' position
        on top of the blankets night

After night like a sentry in wartime or a customs
        inspector at a dangerous border,
                so I never abandoned myself
                to harmonious solitude for fifteen
        more years, until
                I dreamed Marilyn was awaiting me
                in a daffodil pasture, St. Veronica's

Napkin hanging on the wall, Jesus rolling
        His eyes at heaven, with still
                a hill to climb before His own
                crown of thorns, which I found
        in Carolyn Sweeney,
                God knows, marijuana soon after,
                with the same joy of the body's

Heaviness getting hauled against its inner
        primordial affection for gravity,
                its lusty distrust of fire and ashes,
                in directions known only
        by desire and the soul:
                there is never a first time
                for a pleasure that's forever.

Poem Without a Freight Train or a Pocket Watch

As their modesty now proved bothersome
Johnny pawned his box of fabulous lasts.
Each insight contains its own special blindness,
and all the little firsts came shrieking out.

Johnny pawned his box of fabulous lasts.
The heart is torn between practice and theory,
and all the little firsts come shrieking out.
Like some clouds we're just necessarily mistaken.

The heart is torn between practice and theory,
those sharp brilliances the violin kaleidoscopes.
Like some clouds we're just necessarily mistaken.
What's a horse but a mule with a marketing team.

Those sharp brilliances the violin kaleidoscopes.
Susie touched the cardboard, sent a razor through the tape.
What's a horse but a mule with a marketing team.
Knock, knock, who's there?—the ampersands of fear.

Susie touched the cardboard, sent a razor through the tape
while we chose sides and adopted bogus rules.
Knock, knock, who's there?—the ampersands of fear,
that poem without a freight train or a pocket watch.

While we chose sides and adopted bogus rules
Johnny pawned his box of fabulous lasts.
Eyes tossed from their sockets and nipples bloated
all the little firsts came shrieking out.

Swinging Low
   (first tornado)

To sail on wings of corrugated iron's
Damn near as good as being your own big kite—
On a March day when the cold wind was up
And bumped me like a bouncy moving wall,
I went drifting out over the meadow and reached
The burnt-down haybarn where the stones weighed down
Their rusty sheets of heaped-up tin rectangles.
I plucked one piece, then turned broadside to the wind
To be driven sailing, stumbling, onefooting high
And low over the meadow till scraped hands
Lost grip and the sheet of iron went blanging
Away over bluestem, touching lightly or sailing
Like shorebirds by wave-fringe.
                    That was why when I stood
And faced into rain from the funnel-cloud's blast
With my cat under one arm, dog in the other,
And felt the ground leave, the wind taking me up
A long second before we struck and came flying apart,
I wanted to sail, wanted to ride like Elijah high
In the thundering wind in my bodiless weight, my breath
Gone before fear could take it, to look downward
And feel as I started to fall the burnt-out sweet
Under my ribs of the ground dragging me down:
It will come, it still will come, and I know I'll be there.

Blind Date with the Muse

Well, not exactly blind; I knew of her.
I was the needy unknown, worried
about appearance, and what, if anything,
she'd see beneath it. And, sad as this sounds,
it was I who fixed myself up—

I didn't mind being middleman
to the man I longed to be. "Yes," she agreed,
then, "I hope you're not the jealous type."
I lied. She named the time and place,
told me there'd be others, ever and always.

The door was open. And there we all were—
men (and women too), empty-handed
and dressed down, each of us hoping
to please by voice alone. In her big chair
she welcomed or frowned, and one man

she gently touched, as if to say, "Don't
despair, it will be delivered soon."
Even as I hated him, I took heart.
She was the plainest woman I'd ever seen.
I wanted to make her up, but found myself

unable to move. All arrangements
suddenly seemed hers. "You look lonely,"
she said, "a little lost, the kind of man
who writes deathly poems about himself.
Sensitive, too," she added, and laughed.

Thus began the evening the Muse,
that life-long tease, first spoke to me.
"If you want to be any good
you must visit me every day," she said.
And then, "I'm hardly ever home."

First Poem

The bulletin board flutters with a flair
for adventure. What is poetry? In *New World Writing*
I scan the lines "Fuzz clings to the huddle"
and "We rise and leave with Please"
with that odd uppercase P. Doctor Finch
doesn't know, he says, contemporary poetry,
nor does Miss Tupper of the survey course,
so I'm on my own. I have read *On the Road*
and "Howl," and Orlovsky's "Frist Poem" (sic).
Like any red-blooded American boy I am shy
before poets who stand tiptoe on little hills
or bend to flowers, so the Beats are my meat.
Doesn't everyone think academia reeks a bit?
Tacked foursquare to the wall, the flyer
says *Presidio* wants poems at a nickel a line.
One of my professors, David Rakoski,
has walked into the lake, and I am called out,
reporting for the *Fiat Lux*, to shed light on it,
by which is meant adding nothing,
while the Dean reveals his pjs underneath
his shirt—a bit of camaraderie in a crisis.
So I'm off to write a poem, whatever that is,
in pentameter, with rhymes in fourteen lines,
which could be a sonnet if I knew for sure.
I don't want them to know it's my first poem,
so I call it "Ontology, Part II." It's philosophical
and obscure. They buy it. In *Presidio,*
it is crabbed by typographical mistakes,
but I don't care because reality is not enough.
Later I wonder if I wrote it because I thought
David Rakoski had a right to his life,
and if I should have called it "Afterward"
since, by writing it, I was turning posthumous.

When my poem appeared

in a respected and established
national and international magazine
that people could actually buy
on newsstands,
people used the word
"proud," as in, they were
of me,
as if I had
the baby,
enough money,
made peace in the Middle East
and Northern Ireland,
stabbed a stake through
the heart of racism,
wrested power from the bad guys who
didn't deserve it,
sat beside my father through
the moment of death,
found a lover who fought
to keep me;
and when my poem appeared,
I had.

First Books

Splashes of color on the cover,
lettering in wedding invitation script,
the name of the writer infinitesimally small
or so unreadably fancy it's clear
the designer is first-time too,
a novice at computer graphics
volunteering her services, an initiate
auditioning, hawking her wares.

But first-time authors keep
their disappointments
to themselves, preferring to believe
readers will pull them anyway
from bookstore shelves, will order
from Amazon, will forgive
their obviously first-time looks
the way first-time lovers forgive
the fumbling of belts, eyelets, straps,
happy enough to have finally
gotten this far, breathless
at the wonder of the other's
nakedness, sacred places
exposed, clumsy even in their
humbleness. And afterwards

the relief of having
the first time behind them
for the first time, filled
with forgiveness, and later,
alone, giggling at themselves
in a bathroom mirror, spotting
mascara on a nose, curious
if the other noticed a pair
of pimples on a chin—
then suddenly stricken,

afraid this first time
will be the only time
it will ever happen.

First Sunset at Outler's Ranch

If I went there a second time
surely the sunset would seem
no more than a daily scald
of sky that is healed by nightfall.
Horses, chest-high in water
lipping marsh grass
would stumble back to shore.
The pond would not unfurl
in the lengthening light
like a bolt of crushed silk
and roosting birds
would preen lice
not stars
from their wings.

But the first time
when I had left the city's
furnaces, levers and locks,
when I lay in the hammock
and the moist pond air
quickened like a lover's breath,
when the sun sank and all along
the banks horses rose dripping
like gods from the marrow
of the earth, the first
time I said oh this
this is
the world.

Feeding the Worms
for Greg

You think this is going to be about death,
but it's really about being hungry all the time.
It's about craving sweets, even though I don't eat sugar
because of my past history of killing off
pound-bags of candy corn and wedding cookies
so I could puke them up like childhood shame
before my daily descent into a bottle.
It's about having kids when I knew better—three,
with a man who vanished into his creole spices,
polished silver, jazz ringing the glassware,
and the slick smiles of young women ready to serve.
It's about a chafing cat-lick of a marriage
that eventually rubbed me raw, and the divorce,
a bad disease that started as a rash,
and later, a man who kisses me like I'm clean,
like there is nowhere else he wants to go.
It's about telling this man he needs to take Vermox
because at least one of my kids has pinworms,
and how, these days, I hang my head in the toilet
searching shit for signs of parasites
as if they were the threads of my life unraveling
and I could stitch them back together again.
The whole *family* has to be treated, and I can't
figure out a way to tell him this
without implying he's part of the family.
And that might scare him away, the very thought
of being part of a family with worms,
with an eight-year-old who plays Boxcar Children
barefoot in the dirt, baking cakes
of grass and sticks, who pretends her father's dead,
that she could bear to lose her mother too.
Or part of a woman who's spent so much of her life
in the bathroom, on her knees. See,
this is not about death, not yet,
but a love poem, my first.

After the First Snow

Everything is forgiven.
You look for what you'd forgotten, the world
like a phrase, like the glasses you lost
in the seventh grade. You searched and searched.
How did they know, the next spring, these were yours?

The dog stops at a branch fallen from a pine.
It must be dry underneath
and animals hiding there for warmth.
The dog snorts, nose deep in the snow, and again,
to get the small names right,
should they happen to survive.

At the end of the street the hill
becomes a question you want to ask, but the snow
is the pale eyelids of someone sleeping.
Even in cities, by buildings
and around the railroad stations, the homeless,
the half-dead people frighten me
with the secret knowledge of cold
they will not share.

There are no signs of a dog from last summer
struck by a car, rolled, dragging itself to the curb,
and its expression suddenly like a man
more solitary than he can bear,
before the driver could even step out.

Never mind. The snow is a child
calling. It says, the sun is shining,
a clean getaway. This dog,
your simple blind sister, noses her way
from track to joyful track, the outlines
of hope. Here is a curlicue, tracks
like string dropped in the new snow, stopped

and the small outstretched marks of a hawk's wing,
like an angel body, a Japanese sign for longevity.
The deceased was not anyone you know.
There is time to take long walks,
to see the snow among everything, thankful
it was not me, friend, not you.

First Lesson: Winter Trees

These winter trees charcoaled against bare sky,
    a few quick strokes on the papery
       blankness, mean to suggest the mind
    leaping into paper, into sky, not bound
by the body's strict borders. The correspondence
    school instructor writes: *The ancient*
       masters loved to brush the trees
    in autumn, their blossoms fallen.
I've never desired the trees' generous
    flowering, but prefer this austere
       beauty, the few branches nodding
    like...like hair swept over a sleeping
lover's mouth, I almost thought too fast.
    Soon enough these patient alders
       will begin to blossom in their wild
    unremembering to inhabit the jade,
celebratory personae of late summer.
    So the task is simple: to live
       without yearning, to kindle
    this empty acre with trees touched
by winter, to shade them without simile,
    without strain. There: the winter trees.
       Their singular, hushed sufficiency.
    Again. Again. Again. Again. Again.
Now you may begin to sketch the ceaseless winter rain.

The First Stone

The law is plain—
bury her to her neck in soil.
Her belly has betrayed her.
It speaks in gurgles and whimpers.
Just look at the child on her lap.

The child on her lap—
the consequence of nights outside
her husband. Who knew
until her belly spoke? For honor
we'll break her. Gather the stones.

She'll crack, admit her wrongs
to the sun above, to the stones,
to the earth baking around her,
to the circle of women, to men
with the village to consider.

Consider the consequences—
if allowed to live. Her example
will lead to further betrayals
until the soil is pregnant with women.
The law is plain—

have her buried to her neck in sand.
Put the first stone in her husband's hand.

After

Once upon a time
a child made an angel
in the sand.

Her arms traced wings
circling over
her thin body.

The imprint
had all the beauty
of a romanesque angel,

her favorites,
from a time
when men believed

and angels came
when you called
and we felt safe.

Today the bird prints
that cross the angel's body
are bombers

and for the first time
in my life I am afraid
to look at the sea.

Introducing *New Year's SOULUTIONS*, from Saint Terri's Inc.

Before the first war news or pain killers of the year,
Confess. Let the mirror be your priest. *Conscience,*
our specially consecrated champagne face mask,
is guaranteed to relieve the faithful of problem skin,
unburdening pores, with a pleasant authentic sting.
Witness the blameless glow that follows a genuine
Act of Contrition daily throughout the year. Then,
resurrect the fallen muscles of brow, jaw, and neck
to their God-given place in the universe with *Chalice.*
A modern herbal formulation based on ancient Holy Land
beauty secrets, this cosmeticological solution
supplies the same fundamentalist minerals that firmed
the chins of Old Testament prophets and Kings, obviating
the harsh, photo damaging effects of desert extremes.
Plagues, wars, and famines will always be with us,
but they needn't ruin your youthful appearance.
Last, complete your conversion in record time
by an application of *Divine Intervention.* Surely,
The Immaculate Conception was no more miraculous
than Mary's dewy complexion. From stable crèche
to foot of the cross to day of her Assumption,
Our Lady retained the luminous texture of her skin,
and the mystery is preserved in our pure lanolin cream,
hand milked from the sebaceous glands of sheep
grazed solely at sites where the Virgin has appeared.
At last, you too, can materialize your visions.

Skin-deep faith? Don't despair. Deepen your skin.
Purchase the full line of *New Year's SOULUTIONS* today
and receive a free perfume sample of *FrankIncense,*
Saint Terri's trademark Neo-Christian scent.

H. Chic

Horse. *Caballo negro.* Black horse in my hair, death-
gallop between my ear and pillow. I am in a room
unfamiliar, even to the dead. There can't possibly exist

ghosts here. They'd run outside with their lapels
on fire, their comb-overs blowing off like dead skin.
If this is bottom, then let the rocks have me, my teeth

become maraca seeds inside my useless, silent mouth.
A blue-eyed rat keeps me company, sits up and crosses
its legs on the ottoman, removes a cigar from its shirt

pouch and lights up. We watch the smoke swirl to choke
the broken-fingered-severed-ear chandelier. A hung man
swings like a skeleton-fish wind chime. A piñata filled

with doubloons, not the kind from Mardi Gras, but that found
under the tongues of infidels. In my veins, syrup coffee,
an unreeling, minnows spilling out of a huge net. Silver

flickers behind my eyelids. I'm dressed well, I say.
Vestido como un muerto. I have returned from shout land,
a country of interminable barking. Whimpering in this corner,

huddled against my own coldness, I scratch a flea off my arm,
then it jumps up and calls me names. Stay, I urge it, stay
and keep me company. It simply says it is late to its circus

act where it turns tricks for a man who has learned to bleed
in order to feed its million word-fleas. I am like that man,
I say. I have learned to speak in shadows. A hundred crows
making up the form of a man who's learned to devour himself.

My Mother's Body

I never saw my mother's body
only her face and freckled limbs,
the crescent of her back
rising like a moon
over the jewel neckline
of midnite-blue beaded silk.

In the bathhouse she undressed
alone, behind the curtain
or an improvised draping of towels.
Her feet squished in the muck
of the drain. I heard the suction
as she peeled her cold
elastic suit from her body.

Once at 2 a.m., when news
of Father's wreck came,
I saw her nakedness sketched
through a flannel gown:
two brown circles above
and a triangle below smiling
through her hysteria
like a painted clownface.

Tinnitus

In my 56th year,
first indication that
the machine's misbehaving,
wiring gone awry:
my head, a hive of killer Vespas,
small aircraft,
synchronous bells.
I sought answers
from the similarly afflicted
who told me I'd adapt,
it could be worse.
I practiced emptying
my mind like a bowl,
turning its fearful contents
into vapor, visualizing
my breath
a saffron river until
one night—and I cannot tell you why—
respite—or for how long—
the hum in my head
simply the oming of monks
and the greater appliances.

Losing My Hair

It fills my hand
like a small animal, asleep
in a world
it'll never know it came into.

I could name it,
freed from my illness.
I close my eyes, rub it gently
against my face

tangled in my fingers,
soft as silk from a cornfield.

Look, look—I call to my husband
carrying it down the stairs.

Not that I wasn't warned
that one day I'd find it
on my pillows,
in the drain,
on my plate,
in my food.

That morning it started to snow,
nothing that'd cover the ground well enough—

black splintered branches,
strewn all over the yard,

neither wind nor trees.

&

I couldn't bear to wrap it in toilet paper,
throw it out.

I carried some strands to the woods
spread them on the ground

for the birds to lift
into their nests.

I placed some more strands
in an empty hornet's nest,

its gray open mouth welcoming
my hand.

The hornets were gone,
but the birds might come back.

I wrapped the last few strands with some horsehair I'd kept.
A few thick pieces of a rich black mane

I'd pulled riding in fear.

&

Donna, the hair stylist, turns on
the electric clippers,
says, *Hon, do me a favor
and close your eyes.*

She's tall, heavy,
and sweet as white sugar,
hair a teased peroxide
blonde beehive.

Over the phone she'd said
not to worry about anything,

they had wigs—
they would play with me.

The first wig makes me look
like an airline ticketing agent.

The second one drives a school bus.
The third one, curling around my mouth

wants sex. That one couldn't be worn
near an opened oven door.

The dark one, like my mother's hair
loves the rain,

travels well in a small box.
Donna says, *Try this human hair,*

it fits like a silk glove.
But it's short, thick oriental hair,

a gold medalist, figure skater's hair.
Donna says the reason my complexion looks so sallow

is because of all the chemo.
I haven't started my treatments yet.

I leave the yellow of her fitting room.
Truth clips close enough.

Sweeping the floor around my chair, Donna says
After the eyelashes and eyebrows go,

your eyes will need more bang.
And there are pencils for the eyebrows.

Changing

Your unmistakable breasts, plain, finely wrinkled,

Strained but not crushed.
You were no longer shocked out of life

To be naked each time you undressed. And I didn't

Turn my gaze downward. All your beautifulness,
Despite the loose skin hanging

Inches from your bones. And the unshaven legs.

You weren't thinking you could rest against me either,
Even when you tried. Thank you, Mother.

You let me see you unprotected, full of doubt, miserable.

So I could know you were still alive, so I could know
What loving someone looked like.

Verse for First

The first time I was born, it
all happened too late, I
wasn't old enough to appreciate the
moment.

The first time I lost my virginity, a
palpable loss of equanimity
pervaded my soul in that moment.

The first time I grew my pubes,
the first time I tied the tubes:
these moments, like pointillist painting, trace
the first time ever I first saw your face.

The first time I drank my first drink of beer, I
found it interfered with the fun of the
first time I turned twenty-one.

Gratification was too long delayed, the
first time I graduated second grade; when
I first got old, I wished I'd stayed
in that moment.

If only I possessed the means and the mien
To relive those moments for the first time again.

The first time I died, it
all happened too soon, with
no time to bargain or importune, not for a moment.

Elevator

Passing my floor
the elevator rises higher and higher.

I see Death in her gray uniform.

She says nothing to me.
I pretend She's not there:

I'm five years old.
We're on a roller coaster

climbing higher & higher
about to fall.

I brace myself:
The elevator begins to wobble.

She stands by the door.
Waiting.

Confession #1

There in the slick streets,
the clouds lit fluorescent
green by city lights, I watch
again as college girls filter
past in twos and threes, their
short skirts moving in
the breeze like silent bells.
Me, a wanderer slowly
losing to the cold, killing
time after a piano lesson.

My chief malfunction is
and has been memory—
the inability to switch off
the visual echoes that plague
me like an indecent proposal,
the minor-key soundtrack
that accompanies my life-movie.

My parents wave, heading
from the pharmacy across
the way, singing perhaps
the thin strains of a Romany
romance as they lean against
one another, an A of laughter,
such graying amusement.

Then the runaway Lincoln
that went through them,
a lurid sea of tone colors.
No skidding. No blare
of a horn. Me breathing
alien air among the ruthless
stares. Me in my peacoat
on a bench, still waiting,
marking silent measures.

My Corpses

My first and last two corpses felt perhaps the mildest pain in
        passing,
then passed or fell into my curious care. Their curtains drawn,
        the criers gone
to cry elsewhere, we made a trio: a man of middle age and build,
        brought down
by a coronary; an old lady, light and on time; and myself,
        seventeen and solitary
and spending my Saturday nights in the ER. It couldn't have
        been legal, their letting me
take the tubes out, bag the bodies and roll them slowly, with
        youthful ceremony
to the morgue, but I had scarcely seen a cemetery, all the
        funerals were in other families,

and a volunteer is finally one who wants. There was nothing I
        didn't want to know then.
It was disgusting—not the crust around the catheters, the death,
        or in the cool basement room the brain
sliced evenly in a jar, just so, with no one for its witness—but me,
        my formality, meant
to impress the living and larger-than-life and suspect here, where
        I'd been sent
on an errand and erred, plagued by the persistence of form, the
        whiffs of formaldehyde, the infections...
by how it ends, with luck: the heart and spleen removed, the
        soul in sections.

Inquest, By Hand

The body prone—almost flat
on its back, but appearing torqued
      crosswise to the spine

to fit the truncated box.
If not for his face, with cosmetics
      made smooth as wax,

one might say sound asleep, but he's
beyond sound, swathed in the *huzz*
      of refrigerated blooms.

Crescents of reflected light
behind lids they closed
      part-way.

A coroner would know
a human hand could be
      so cold:

suddenly alone with the body in state,
for no reason per se I took
      that hand in mine

and held on. Embalmed, the thing was like
a metal knob in sub-frozen December,
      each molecule of warmth

sucked away as what I clasped
took my pulse and flung it
      to ground, zeroed at root.

As cold moved upward via the blood
in my arm, I was waiting
      —for what?

Incubus and succubus, no longer incarnadine,
one body above and the other beneath.
        A mystic will warn

your *pneuma* can be squandered,
stolen by a reckless touch.
        But I held on.

Enormous deletion, smothered in propane
while lacing his boots. The dead boy's hand
        larger than my own,

rimed with calluses from pencils and pliers,
a hand I never grasped alive
        with *Salut—Ça va?*

My fingers, palm, and forearm gone numb.
Waiting for a sign from within or without,
        in his tongue or mine.

Instead *Hush* went the ventilators, sucked wind
from below, chilling us to stillness.
        The cadaver was quiet.

About the Editor

Laure-Anne Bosselaar grew up in Belgium and moved to the United States in 1987. Fluent in four languages, she has also published poems in French and Flemish. She is the author of *The Hour Between Dog and Wolf* and *Small Gods of Grief,* which won the Isabella Gardner Prize for Poetry for 2001; both books are published by BOA Editions.

With her husband, poet Kurt Brown, she edited *Night Out: Poems about Hotels, Motels, Restaurants and Bars.* She is the editor of *Outsiders: Poems About Rebels Exiles and Renegades*, as well as *Urban Nature: Poems about Wildlife in the City.*

She and Kurt Brown have completed a book of translations from Flemish poet Herman de Coninck: *The Plural of Happiness*, which the Field Translations Series will publish in 2006.

She teaches a graduate poetry workshop at Sarah Lawrence College.

Biographical Notes

Kim Addonizio's latest collection *What Is This Thing Called Love* was published by W.W. Norton in 2004. She is also co-author, with Dorianne Laux, of *The Poet's Companion: A Guide to the Pleasures of Writing Poetry* (W.W. Norton).

Joan Aleshire has taught in the MFA Program for Writers at Warren Wilson College since 1983. Her two latest books, *The Yellow Transparents* (1997*)* and *Litany of Thanks* (2003*)*, were published by Four Way Books. She lives in Shrewsbury, Vermont.

Ellen Bass's most recent book, *Mules of Love* (BOA Editions) received the Lambda Literary Award for Poetry. She teaches poetry and creative writing in Santa Cruz.

Robin Becker, Professor of English and Women's Studies at Penn State University, has published five collections of poems including *The Horse Fair* and serves as poetry editor for *The Women's Review of Books*.

Marvin Bell's most recent book of poetry is *Rampant* (2004). For forty years, he served on the faculty of the Writers' Workshop at the University of Iowa. For two decades he has lived each year in at least three locations: Sag Harbor, New York; Iowa City, Iowa; and Port Townsend, Washington, a mobile existence he and his wife call "tricoastal."

Bruce Berger is the author of numerous books on the intersection of nature and culture, including *The Telling Distance*, winner of the Western States Book Award, and *Almost an Island*. His poems have appeared in *Poetry*, *Barron's*, *The New York Times* and various reviews, and have been collected in *Facing the Music* (Confluence Press, 1995).

Sophie Cabot Black's first poetry collection, *The Misunderstanding of Nature*, received the Poetry Society of America's Norma Farber First Book Award. *The Descent*, a second collection of poems, was published by Graywolf Press in the fall of 2004. She currently teaches at Columbia.

Joel Brouwer is the author of *Exactly What Happened* (Purdue University Press, 1999) and *Centuries* (Four Way Books, 2003). He has held fellowships from the NEA and the Mrs. Giles Whiting Foundation. He teaches at the University of Alabama.

Kurt Brown's most recent poetry collection is *Fables from the Ark* (Custom Words, 2004). His fourth book *Future Ship* will come out from Story Line Press in 2005. He is the editor of four anthologies, as well as a book of essays *The Measured Word: On Poetry and Science*, (University of Georgia Press). He teaches at Sarah Lawrence College.

Susan Browne's *Buddha's Dogs* was selected as the winner of the Four Way Books Intro Prize in Poetry by Edward Hirsch and published in 2004. She teaches literature and writing at Diablo Valley College in Pleasant Hill, California.

Andrea Hollander Budy is the author of *The Other Life* and *House Without a Dreamer* which received the Nicholas Roerich Poetry Prize. She is the Writer-in-Residence at Lyon College.

Christine Casson has completed *Grace*, a manuscript of poems, and is working on a study of the poetic sequence titled *Sequence and Time Signature: A Study in Poetic Orchestration*. She is Scholar/Writer-in-Residence at Emerson College.

Peter Cooley has published seven books of poetry, six of them with Carnegie Mellon, the last being *A Place Made of Starlight*. Originally from the Midwest, he has lived in New Orleans and taught creative writing at Tulane since 1975.

Miles A. Coon is the director of the Palm Beach Poetry Festival. He's been married to Mimi for over forty years and has two adult children and a granddaughter of fourteen months. His work has appeared or is forthcoming in *BigCityLit*, *Long Island Quarterly*, *Lumina*, *Rattapallax* and in *Key West: A Collection*.

Mark Cox teaches in the Department of Creative Writing at the University of North Carolina Wilmington. His honors include an award from the Mrs. Giles Whiting Foundation. His latest books are *Thirty Seven Years from the Stone* (Pitt Poetry Series, 1998), and *Natural Causes*, (Pitt Poetry Series, 2004).

Silvia Curbelo's most recent collection of poems, *Ambush*, won the Main Street Rag Chapbook Contest. She is the author of two previous collections, *The Secret History of Water*, (Anhinga Press) and *The Geography of Leaving* (Silverfish Review Press). A native of Cuba, Silvia lives in Tampa, Florida, and is managing editor for *Organica* magazine.

Debra Kang Dean is the author of *Precipitates* (BOA, 2003) and *News of Home* (BOA, 1998). She is a contributing editor for *Tar River Poetry*.

Deborah DeNicola edited the anthology *Orpheus & Company; Contemporary Poems on Greek Mythology.* She is the author of *Where Divinity Begins* (Alice James Books) and two chapbooks.

Stephen Dunn's latest collection is *The Insistence of Beauty.* His book *Different Hours* was the winner of the Pulitzer Prize in 2001. In 1995 Dunn received an Academy Award in Literature from the American Academy of Arts and Letters. He divides his time between Frostburg, Maryland, and Pomona, New Jersey, where he is a Distinguished Professor of Creative Writing at Richard Stockton College.

Ron Egatz received the Glimmer Train Poetry Award, the Greenburgh Poetry Award, and was a runner-up for the Grolier Poetry Prize. He lives near Manhattan, where he is editorial director of Camber Press.

Roger Fanning's first book of poems *The Island Itself* was a National Poetry Series selection. His second book of poems *Homesick* was published by Penguin Putnam in 2002. He is currently at work on a third collection and lives in Seattle with his wife and son.

Beth Ann Fennelly's first book, *Open House*, received the 2001 Kenyon Review Prize. Her second book, *Tender Hooks*, was published by W.W. Norton in 2004. She has received fellowships from the NEA and at the Bread Loaf Writers' Conference. She is an assistant professor of English at the University of Mississippi.

Vievee Francis's poems have appeared in *Callaloo, Crab Orchard Poetry Review*, and the *2003 Grolier Prize Annual.* "The First Stone" is part of her manuscript, *Heart of Palm.*

Sanford Fraser's poems have appeared in *Barrow Street, Mudfish, The New Laurel Review, The New York Quarterly, Turnstile*, and *Wind*, as well as several magazines in France. In 2005, his book of poems *Among Strangers I've Known All My Life* will be published by Tarabuste Editions in France.

Richard Frost's most recent collection is *Neighbor Blood* (Sarabande Books). He is Professor of English at the State University College, Oneonta, New York.

Tseverin Furey lives in Rhode Island, where he paints, composes and sings his own songs, and works on several fiction and non-fiction book projects. He graduated from the University of Michigan's MFA program in creative writing (fiction). He is a published cartoonist and essayist; "Verse for First" is his first published poem.

Tony Gloeggler is the author of *One on One*, which won the 1998 Pearl Poetry Prize, *One Wish Left* (Pavement Saw Press) and *My Other Life* (Jane Street Press). He is a native of New York City and currently manages a group home for developmentally disabled men in Brooklyn.

Douglas Goetsch is the author of *The Job of Being Everybody* (Cleveland State University Press, 2004), *Nobody's Hell* (Hanging Loose Press, 1999) and three award-winning chapbooks. He currently runs a creative writing program for incarcerated teens at Passages Academy in the South Bronx.

Jennifer Grotz is the author of *Cusp* (Houghton Mifflin, 2003) and a limited-edition chapbook *Not Body* (Urban Editions, 2001).

Kimiko Hahn is the author of six collections of poetry including *The Artist's Daughter* (W.W. Norton), *Mosquito and Ant* (W.W. Norton), and *Earshot* (Hanging Loose Press), which received the Theodore Roethke Memorial Poetry Prize and an Association of Asian American Studies Literature Award.

Adam Halbur grew up in the rural communities of Dodge and Monroe counties, Wisconsin, and now lives with his wife and young son near Minneapolis. He holds an MFA degree in Creative Writing from Warren Wilson College in Asheville, North Carolina.

Mark Halliday teaches at Ohio University. His books of poems are: *Little Star* (1987), *Tasker Street* (1992), *Selfwolf* (1999), and *Jab* (2002).

Jeffrey Harrison is the author of three books of poetry, *The Singing Underneath* (1988), *Signs of Arrival* (1996), and *Feeding the Fire* (Sarabande, 2001). He has received fellowships from the Guggenheim Foundation and the NEA. His poems have appeared in *The New Republic, The New Yorker, The Paris Review, Poetry, The Yale Review,* and *Poets of the New Century*.

Edward Hirsch is the author of six books of poems including his most recent *Lay Back the Darkness* (Alfred A. Knopf, 2003). He has been a professor of English at Wayne State University and the University of Houston. Hirsch is currently the president of the John Simon Guggenheim Memorial Foundation.

Steven Huff's first book of poems, *The Water We Came From*, was published in 2003 by FootHills Publishing. The former publisher and managing editor of BOA Editions, he is now a freelance editor and writer.

Barbara Hurd is the author of *Entering the Stone: On Caves and Feeling Through the Dark* (Houghton Mifflin, 2003), *The Singer's Temple* (Bright Hill Press, 2003), *Stirring the Mud: On Swamps, Bogs, and Human Imagination*, a *Los Angeles Times* Best Book of 2001 (Beacon), and *Objects in this Mirror* (Artscape, 1994). She teaches creative writing at Frostburg State University in Frostburg, Maryland.

Colette Inez has been on the faculty of Columbia University's undergraduate writing program since 1983. She has received a Guggenheim, two NEAs and a Rockefeller Foundation fellowship. Her most recent books are a memoir, *The Secret of M. Dulong* (University of Wisconsin Press, 2005) and a book of poems, *Spinoza Doesn't Live Here Anymore* (Melville House Books, 2004).

Gray Jacobik's book, *The Double Task* (University of Massachusetts Press, 1998) received the Juniper Prize. *The Surface of Last Scattering* (Texas Review Press, 1999) was selected by X. J. Kennedy for the X. J. Kennedy Poetry Prize. *Brave Disguises* won the AWP Award Series in poetry (University of Pittsburgh Press, 2002). She is a member of the faculty of the Stonecoast MFA Program.

Eric Johnson is a student in the MFA Program for Writers at Warren Wilson College. His work has appeared in the *Atlanta Review* and the *Greensboro Review*. He currently lives in San Diego where he teaches English.

Kate Johnson is the author of three books of poetry, the most recent of which, *Wind Somewhere, and Shade*, received a Gradvia Award from NAAP. Kate teaches at Sarah Lawrence College where she directs the MFA Program in Poetry. She has a private practice in psychoanalysis in Bedford Hills, New York.

A. Van Jordan is the author of *Rise,* which received the PEN/Oakland Josephine Miles Book Award, and of *M-A-C-N-O-L-I-A* (W.W. Norton). In 2004, he was the recipient of a Whiting Award. He is Assistant Professor of English at the University of North Carolina at Greensboro, and on the faculty of the MFA Program for Writers at Warren Wilson College.

Meg Kearney's *An Unkindness of Ravens*, was published by BOA Editions in 2001. She has been featured on Poetry Daily, and her work has appeared in numerous publications, including *Agni*, *Ploughshares*, and *Poetry*, and the anthologies *Where Icarus Falls*, *Urban Nature*, and *The Poets' Grimm*. She teaches poetry at The New School University, and is acting executive director of the National Book Foundation.

David Keller's most recent book is titled *Trouble in History* (White Pine Press, 2000). He serves as director of admissions for the annual Frost Place Festival of Poetry, held in Franconia, New Hampshire, and is married to the poet Eloise Bruce.

Wendy Wilder Larsen has had poems published in *Confrontation*, *The Paris Review*, *Tendril*, and *13th Moon*. Her poems have also appeared in anthologies including *The KGB Bar Book of Poems, Outsiders, Women on War*, and *A Year in Poetry*. Her book *Shallow Graves*, a verse novel about Vietnam, was published by Random House. She is on the board of Poets House.

Dorianne Laux is the author of *Awake* (1990), *What We Carry* (1994), a finalist for the National Book Critics Circle Award, and *Smoke*, all published by BOA Editions. Her new book *Facts About the Moon* is published by W.W. Norton. She is also co-author, with Kim Addonizio, of *The Poet's Companion: A Guide to the Pleasures of Writing Poetry* (W.W. Norton, 1997). Laux teaches in the University of Oregon's creative writing program.

David Dodd Lee is the author of *Downsides of Fish Culture* (New Issues Press, 1997), *Arrow Pointing North* (Four Way Books, 2002) and *Abrupt Rural* (New Issues Press, 2004). He has been poetry editor at *Passages North* and *Third Coast*. With Donna Munro, he is editor of Half Moon Bay poetry chapbooks. He works as a freelance editor and poetry coach, and is editor-in-chief of the annual anthology *SHADE*.

Philip Levine was born in 1928 in Detroit and attended Wayne University (now Wayne State University). He has received the National Book Award for *What Work Is* (1991) and the Pulitzer Prize for *The Simple Truths* (1995). His most recent book is *Breath* (Random House, 2004).

Larry Levis was professor of Creative Writing at Virginia Commonwealth University at the time of his death in 1996. His first book, *Wrecking Crew*, received the United States Award of the International Poetry Forum. His second book, *The Afterlife*, received the Lamont Award in 1976. In 1981, *The Dollmaker's Ghost* was a winner of the open competition of the National Poetry Series. His last work, *Elegy*, was published posthumously in 1997.

Deena Linett is Professor of English at Montclair State University. Her first poetry collection, *Rare Earths*, appeared in 2001 from BOA Editions; they will bring out her new book *Woman Crossing a Field* in late 2005.

John Logan was awarded the Lenore Marshall Prize by the New Hope Foundation and *The Nation,* as well as the William Carlos Williams Award by the Poetry Society of America for *The Bridge of Change: Poems 1974-1980* and *Only the Dreamer Can Change the Dream: Selected Poems,* both published in 1981. BOA Editions published his *Collected Poems* in 1989.

James Longenbach is the author of two books of poems, *Threshold* and *Fleet River,* both published by the University of Chicago Press. He is also the author of several books about contemporary poetry, most recently *The Resistance to Poetry.* He teaches in the Warren Wilson MFA Program for Writers and at the University of Rochester, where he is Joseph H. Gilmore Professor of English.

Thomas Lux holds the Bourne Chair in Poetry and is the director of the McEver Visiting Writers Program at the Georgia Institute of Technology. He has been awarded three NEA fellowships and the Kingsley Tufts Award and is a former Guggenheim Fellow. He lives in Atlanta.

Anne Marie Macari received the APR/Honickman first book prize in 2000 for *Ivory Cradle.* Macari is on the core faculty of the New England College Low Residency MFA Program. Her new book, *Gloryland,* will be published in 2005 by Alice James Books.

Peter Makuck is the author of five volumes of poems and has edited *Tar River Poetry* at East Carolina University for twenty-five years. His second collection of short fiction, *Costly Habits,* published by the University of Missouri Press, was nominated for a PEN/Faulkner Award. *Off Season in the Promised Land,* a volume of poems, will be published by BOA Editions, in fall 2005.

Karen McCosker lives in northern Maine where she works as a lecturer and tutor at the University of Maine at Presque Isle. She is the editor of *A Poem a Day,* an anthology of poetry meant to encourage the learning of poems by heart.

Jeffrey McDaniel is the author of three books, most recently *The Splinter Factory.* He teaches at Sarah Lawrence College.

Joe-Anne McLaughlin's book *Jam* (2001) is available from BOA Editions. She lives in Munnsville, New York.

Erika Meitner's first collection of poems, *Inventory at the All-Night Drugstore,* received the 2002 Anhinga Prize. She holds an MFA from the University of Virginia, where she was a Hoyns Fellow, and is working on her doctoral degree in Religion there as the Morgenstern Fellow in Jewish Studies.

Joseph Millar is the author of *Overtime* (2001) which was a finalist for the Oregon Book Award. He is the recipient of a 2003 NEA Fellowship in poetry. Formerly a telephone installation foreman and commercial fisherman, he now teaches at Oregon State University.

Carol Moldaw is the author of three books of poetry: *The Lightning Field*, winner of the 2002 FIELD Poetry Prize, *Chalkmarks on Stone*, and *Taken from the River*, as well as a chapbook, *Through the Window*. She lives in Pojoaque, New Mexico.

Peter E. Murphy's poems and essays have appeared in *The American Book Review, Beloit Poetry Journal, Commonweal, The Shakespeare Quarterly, Witness, World Order*, and elsewhere. He has received fellowships from The Folger Shakespeare Library, The National Endowment for the Humanities, Yaddo, and the White House Commission on Presidential Scholars.

D. Nurkse is the author of eight books of poetry, including *Burnt Island* (forthcoming), *The Fall, The Rules of Paradise, Leaving Xaia*, and *Voices over Water*. He received the 2003 Frederick Bock Prize from *Poetry*.

Anne-Marie Oomen is the author of *Pulling Down the Barn*, a memoir, and two chapbooks of poetry, *Seasons of the Sleeping Bear* and *Moniker* with Ray Nargis. She edited *Looking Over My Shoulder: Reflections on the Twentieth Century*, a collection of older adult writings, and serves as Chair of Creative Writing at Interlochen Arts Academy.

Dzvinia Orlowsky is a founding editor of *Four Way Books* and teaches in the Stonecoast MFA Program for Creative Writing at the University of Southern Maine. She has published three collections with Carnegie Mellon University Press, most recently *Except for One Obscene Brushstroke* (2004). Her translations of contemporary Ukrainian writing including Alexander Dovzhenko's *The Enchanted Desna* have appeared in numerous magazines and anthologies.

Benjamin Paloff's poems have appeared in *Boston Review, Harvard Review, The New Republic, The Paris Review*, and elsewhere. A literary translator—most recently of Dorota Masłowska's *White and Red* (Grove Press)—he is also a contributor to such publications as *The Nation* and *The New Leader*. He is currently a PhD candidate at Harvard.

Alan Michael Parker is the author of three books of poetry, including *Love Song with Motor Vehicles* (BOA, 2003), and a novel, *Cry Uncle* (University Press of Mississippi, 2005). He teaches at Davidson College and in the Queens University low-residency MFA program.

Ricardo Pau-Llosa has published five books of poetry, the last three from Carnegie Mellon: *Cuba* (1993), *Vereda Tropical* (1999), and *The Mastery Impulse* (2003). He is also a widely published art critic specializing in Latin American art.

Patrick Phillips' first book, *Chattahoochee*, was published by the University of Arkansas Press in 2004. His honors include a "Discovery" / *The Nation* Award, the Sjoberg Translation Prize of the American-Scandinavian Foundation, and a Fulbright Scholarship at the University of Copenhagen. He is currently a MacCracken Fellow at NYU.

Browning Porter grew up in rural Catharpin, Virginia. Now he lives in Charlottesville, where he makes his living as a graphic artist and no living whatsoever as a singer in the folk duo Nickeltown. He has an MFA in poetry from Warren Wilson College, and he founded the Charlottesville Writing Center.

Carter Revard grew up on the Osage Reservation in Oklahoma, where a tornado came by on a Sunday in 1942. After working as farm hand and greyhound trainer, he holds BAs from the University of Tulsa and Oxford (Rhodes Scholarship) and a PhD from Yale; he taught medieval and American Indian literatures until he retired in 1997. His books include *Ponca War Dancers*; *Cowboys and Indians Christmas Shopping*; *An Eagle Nation*; *Family Matters, Tribal Affairs*; and *Winning the Dust Bowl*.

Carlos Reyes, a poet, translator, and writer who lives in Portland, Oregon, travels frequently to interesting places such as Ireland, Spain and Ecuador. His latest book of poems is *At the Edge of the Western Wave* (Lost Horse Press, 2004). He has translated into English the *Obra Completa Poetica / The Complete Poetic Works* of Jorge Carrera Andrade, Ecuador's preeminent poet of the 20th century, which was published in 2004 in Ecuador.

Katrina Roberts is Associate Professor of English/Creative Writing at Whitman College. Her first book *How Late Desire Looks* received the Peregrine Smith Prize in 1997. The University of Washington Press will publish a second book of poems, *The Quick*, in Fall 2005.

Len Roberts is the author of eight books of poetry, most recently *The Silent Singer: New and Selected Poems* (University of Illinois Press, 2001). BOA Editions will publish his second book of translations of the great Hungarian poet, Sandor Csoori—titled *Before and After the Fall: New Poems by Sandor Csoori*—in June, 2004.

Tania Rochelle received her BA in English from the University of Georgia and graduated from the MFA Program for Writers at Warren Wilson College. She teaches creative writing at Portfolio Center, in Atlanta, and lives in Marietta, Georgia, with her husband and four children. Her first book, *Karaoke Funeral*, was awarded the Violet Reed Haas Prize, sponsored by Snake Nation Press, and was published in the fall of 2003.

Matthew Rohrer is the author of *A Hummock in the Malookas*, a selection of the National Poetry Series; *Satellite*; *Nice Hat. Thanks* (with Joshua Beckman); the audio *CD Adventures While Preaching the Gospel of Beauty*; and *A Green Light*. He grew up in Oklahoma and attended universities in Ann Arbor; Dublin, Ireland; and Iowa City. He lives in Brooklyn and is a poetry editor of Fence Magazine and Fence Books.

Kenneth Rosen's *The Origins Of Tragedy*, CavanKerry, is free, signed by the author, to whomever asks for it in two bookstores and conveys this accomplishment to Rosen, in Portland, Maine, isolated as an onion, with an aging, conspicuously inadequate exterior (Rosen, a Virgo, recently turned 64), unclear layers and layers which bring tears to the eyes yet exude an aroma that makes others gag and catch their breath, and an absurdly delicate, virginal green interior.

J. Allyn Rosser's books are *Misery Prefigured* (Crab Orchard Award, 2001) and *Bright Moves* (Morse Prize, 1990). She has received fellowships from the NEA, the Ohio Arts Council, and the New Jersey State Council on the Arts, and the Peter I.B. Lavan Younger Poets Award from the Academy of American Poets. She teaches at Ohio University.

Vern Rutsala lives in Portland, Oregon, where he is a professor of English at Lewis and Clark College. His poetry collections include *The Window, Laments, The Journey Begins, Paragraphs, Walking Home from the Icehouse, Backtracking,* and *Selected Poems* (Story Line Press).

Michael Ryan is the author of four books of poems, an autobiography, a memoir, and a collection of essays about poetry and writing. The memoir, *Baby B* (Graywolf), and *New and Selected Poems* (Houghton Mifflin) were both published in Spring, 2004. He is Professor of English and Creative Writing at the University of California, Irvine.

Nicholas Samaras received the 1992 Yale Series of Younger Poets Award for his first book, *Hands of the Saddlemaker*. He was awarded a Fellowship from the Lilly Endowment Foundation to spend the summer of 2004 in Greece, attending and writing about the Olympics.

Jim Schley, who lives in Vermont, has been co-editor of *New England Review* and editor of the book *Writing in a Nuclear Age* (University Press of New England, 1984). His poetry chapbook *One Another* was published by Chapiteau Press (1999, www.chapiteau.org).

Grace Schulman's latest poetry collections are *The Paintings of Our Lives* (2001) and *Days of Wonder: New and Selected Poems* (2002, both Houghton Mifflin). Recent awards include a Guggenheim Fellowship; the Aiken Taylor Award for Poetry; and the Distinguished Alumna Award, New York University. She is the editor of *The Poems of Marianne Moore* (Viking 2003) and Distinguished Professor of English, Baruch College, C.U.N.Y.

Peter Sears received the 1999 Peregrine Smith Poetry Prize for his manuscript *The Brink*, which was published by Gibbs-Smith and subsequently awarded the 2000 Western States Book Award in poetry. Sears founded the Oregon Literary Coalition in 1997 and co-founded, with Kim Stafford, Friends of William Stafford in 1999. He lives with his wife in Corvallis, Oregon.

Tim Seibles is the author of *Hammerlock*, *Body Moves* and *Hurdy-Gurdy*. His newest collection, *Buffalo Head Solos*, was released by the Cleveland State University Poetry Center in 2004. He lives in Norfolk, Virginia, where he teaches at Old Dominion.

Jason Shinder's recent poetry book is *Among Women* (Graywolf Press). His forthcoming books include *True Minds: The Letters of Jack Kerouac and Allen Ginsberg* and *Hollywood Poets: Filmmakers and their Favorite Poems*. Founder of the YMCA National Writer's Voice and the Sundance Institute's Writing Program, he teaches at Bennington College's MFA program and is Visiting Poet at the Hellenistic Institute in Greece.

Enid Shomer has published four collections, most recently *Stars at Noon: Poems from the Life of Jacqueline Cochran*. The recipient of two grants from the NEA, the Eunice Tietjens Prize from *Poetry*, and other awards, Shomer edits the University of Arkansas Press Poetry Series.

Gerald Stern is the author of thirteen books of poetry including, *This Time: New and Selected Poems*, which won the National Book Award in 1998, and most recently *American Sonnets,* published in 2002, both from Norton. A collection of personal essays titled *What I Can't Bear Losing: Notes From a Life* was released in the fall of 2003.

Norman Stock is the author of *Buying Breakfast for My Kamikaze Pilot* (Gibbs Smith, 1994), winner of the Peregrine Smith Poetry Contest.

Virgil Suárez was born in Havana, Cuba, in 1962. Since 1974 he has lived in the United States. His most recent books are *Infinite Refuge*, *Palm Crows*, *Banyan*, *Guide to the Blue Tongue*, and *90 Miles: Selected and New Poems*. He is the co-editor of four anthologies published by the University of Iowa Press: *American Diaspora*, *Like Thunder*, *Vespers*, and *Red, White, and Blue*.

Karen Swenson was born in New York, educated at Barnard College, and still lives in the city. Her first book was published by Doubleday, *An Attic of Ideals*. Her last two books, including her new and selected, *A Daughter's Latitude*, were published by Copper Canyon Press. Her next book, *What Woman Has a Country?* will also be published by Copper Canyon.

Arthur Sze is the author of seven books of poetry, including *The Redshifting Web: Poems 1970-1998*, and *The Silk Dragon: Translations from the Chinese*. A new collection of poems, *Quipu*, will be published by Copper Canyon Press in 2005. He lives in Santa Fe, New Mexico, and teaches at the Institute of American Indian Arts.

Daniel Tobin is the author of *Where the World is Made*, *Double Life*, and *The Narrows*. Among his awards are a "Discovery"/*The Nation* Award, The Robert Penn Warren Award, a creative writing fellowship from the NEA, and the Robert Frost Fellowship.

Ryan Van Cleave's most recent books include a poetry collection, *The Magical Breasts of Britney Spears* (Pavement Saw, 2004), and a creative writing textbook, *Contemporary American Poetry: Behind the Scenes* (Allyn & Bacon/Longman, 2003). He lives in upstate South Carolina.

Thom Ward is editor for BOA Editions, Ltd. He teaches creative writing workshops at elementary and high schools. He is the author of two collections from Carnegie Mellon, *Small Boat With Oars of Different Size* and, in 2004, *Various Orbits*. His chapbook, *Tumblekid*, was the winner of the 1998 Devil's Millhopper Poetry Contest.

Michael Waters teaches at Salisbury University and in the New England College MFA Program in Poetry. In spring 2005 he was Stadler Poet-in-Residence at Bucknell. His most recent collection is *Parthenopi: New and Selected Poems* (BOA Editions, 2001).

Ellen Doré Watson's third collection, *Ladder Music*, received the New York/New England Award from Alice James Books. Other honors include a Massachusetts Cultural Council Artists Grant, the Rona Jaffe Writers' Award, and a NEA Translation Fellowship to translate the work of Brazilian poet Adélia Prado. An editor at *The Massachusetts Review* and director of the Poetry Center at Smith College, Watson lives with her daughter in Conway, Massachusetts.

Afaa Michael Weaver (b. Michael S. Weaver) is the author of nine collections of poetry, including *Multitudes*. As a playwright his latest play is *Berea*. He is the Alumnae Professor of English at Simmons College.

Charles Harper Webb's most recent book of poems, *Tulip Farms and Leper Colonies*, was published in 2001 by BOA Editions. In 2002, the University of Iowa Press published *Stand Up Poetry: An Expanded Anthology*, edited by Webb. Recipient of grants from the Whiting and Guggenheim foundations, he teaches at California State University, Long Beach.

Estha Weiner is co-editor and contributor to *Blues for Bill: A Tribute to William Matthews*, forthcoming from Akron Poetry Series. Her poems have appeared or are forthcoming in the anthology *The Poets Grimm* (Story Line Press), and in such magazines as *Barrow Street* and *The New Republic*.

M.L. Williams' publications include *How Much Earth: The Fresno Poets* (with Christopher Buckley and David Oliveira). He teaches creative writing at Valdosta State University and is poetry editor for the *Snake Nation Review*.

Peter Wood's poems have appeared in national and regional journals and anthologies since 1968. He has usually played a role in the poetry festivals of the Robert Frost Museum (Franconia, NH) and the Geraldine R. Dodge Foundation (Waterloo Village, NJ). In 2001, Wood retired from The College of New Jersey where he taught poetry and writing for most of his career.

Baron Wormser is the author of six books of poetry and the co-author of two books about teaching poetry. He lives with his wife in Hallowell, Maine.

Matthew Zapruder's first collection of poems, *American Linden*, was the winner of the Tupelo Press Editors' Prize (2002). He is the co-translator of *Secret Weapon*, the final collection by the late Romanian poet Eugen Jebeleanu. Currently he is the Editor of Verse Press and an instructor of Creative Writing at the New School in New York City.

Copyright Pages

204

John Logan, "The Picnic" from John Logan: The Collected Poems (BOA Editions 1990). Copyright © 1990 by John Logan. Reprinted by permission of BOA Editions Ltd.

James Longenbach, "Orphic Night" from *Fleet River* (University of Chicago Press, 2003). Copyright © 2004 by James Longenbach. Reprinted with permission from the University of Chicago. All rights reserved.

Thomas Lux, "Upon Seeing an Ultrasound Photo of an Unborn Child" from the *Drowned River* (Houghton Mifflin, 1990) Copyright © 1990 by Thomas Lux. Reprinted with permission from the author.

Anne Marie Macari, "New York, 1927" from *American Poetry Review* No. 6 Vol. 1 (Nov./Dec. 2002). Copyright © 2002 by Anne Marie Macari. Reprinted with permission from the author.

Peter Makuck, "Story of a Sound" from *The Sunken Lightship* (BOA Editions, Ltd., 1990). Copyright © 2002 by Peter Makuck. Reprinted with permission from BOA Editions, Ltd.

Karen McCosker, "Tinnitus" Copyright © 2004 by Karen McCosker. Printed with permission from the author.

Jeffrey McDaniel, "The First One" from *The Forgiveness Parade* (Manic D Press, 1998). Copyright © 1998 by Jeffrey McDaniel. Reprinted with permission from Manic D Press.

Joe-Anne McLaughlin, "Introducing New Year's SOULUTIONS, from Saint Terri's Inc." Copyright © 2004 by Joe-Anne McLaughlin. Printed with permission from the author.

Erica Meitner, "All the Pools in Queens" from *Inventory at the All-Night Drugstore* (Anhinga Press, 2003). Copyright © 2003 by Anhinga Press. Reprinted with permission from Anhinga Press.

Erica Meitner, "Job" from *Inventory at the All-Night Drugstore* (Anhinga Press, 2003). Copyright © 2003 by Anhinga Press. Reprinted with permission from Anhinga Press.

Joseph Millar, "Poem for a New Girlfriend" Copyright © 2004 by Joseph Millar. Printed with permission from the author.

Carol Moldaw, "The Widening" Copyright © 2004 by Carol Moldaw. Printed with permission from the author.

Peter E. Murphy, "Sequence" from *Stubborn Child* (Jane Street Press, New York, NY) by Peter E. Murphy, Copyright © 2005. Reprinted by permission from the author.

Peter E. Murphy, "Learning to Swim at Poverty Beach" from *Stubborn Child* (Jane Street Press, New York, NY) by Peter E. Murphy, Copyright © 2005. Reprinted by permission from the author.

Tania@portfoliocenter.com